ALEISTER CROWLEY AND THE OUIJA BOARD

by J. Edward Cornelius

Feral House

Aleister Crowley and the Ouija Board
©2005 by J. Edward Cornelius

ISBN: 1-932595-10-4

10 9 8 7 6 5 4 3 2

Feral House
1240 W. Sims Way Suite 124
Port Towsend, WA 98368

www.feralhouse.com

Cover design by Sean Tejaratchi

INTRODUCTION

Many readers consider the Ouija board either a child's game or equate it with the movement of Spiritualism. We shall examine the history of the Board in the latter's regard simply because, prior to Spiritualism, the use of a talking board remained relatively unknown, even though it had been used for centuries around the world in one form or another. Spiritualism brought the talking board into the forefront of mainstream society. However, there is a major difference between the board's application amongst Spiritualists and its use by Magicians that can be summed up by a single word: *Will!*

The spiritualistic phenomenon is often the product of a trance state. Most of the materializations are considered a by-product of a passive relationship between a medium and the board. Spiritualists often pride themselves in exerting no conscious control over that which they're channeling. Magicians, on the other hand, perform their rites consciously, deliberately and with the full intent of their Will. While they might assume a passive, mediumistic role when working a Ouija board, they remain very active in their ability to control that which is manifesting. From the start it is important for you, the reader, to distinguish between the simple children's game, Spiritualism's usage, and Aleister Crowley's approach to this subject of the talking board. This book is primarily concerned with the latter.

Many people may be unaware that Aleister Crowley advocated the Ouija board's use. Jane Wolfe, who lived with Crowley at his infamous Abbey of Cefalu, also used the Ouija board. She credits some of her greatest spiritual communications to use of this implement. Crowley also discussed the Ouija board with another of his students, Frater Achad (Charles Stansfeld Jones); it is frequently mentioned in their unpublished letters. Throughout 1917 Achad experimented with the board as a means of summoning Angels, as opposed to Elementals. In one letter Crowley told Jones, "Your Ouija board experiment is rather fun. You see how very satisfactory it is, but I believe things improve greatly with practice. I think you should keep to one angel, and make the magical preparations more elaborate."

Over the next few years both became so fascinated with the board that they discussed marketing their own design. Their discourse culminated in a letter, dated February 21, 1919, in which Crowley tells Jones, "Re: Ouija Board. I offer you the position of my confidential agent in this matter, on the basis of ten percent of my net profit. You are, if you accept this, responsible for the legal protection of the ideas, and the marketing of the copyrighted designs. I trust that this may be satisfactory to you. I hope to let you have the material in the course of a week..." In March, Crowley wrote to Achad to inform him, "I'll think up another name for Ouija." But their business venture never came to fruition and Crowley's new design, along with his name for the board, has not survived.

This book begins by studying the board's history, its basic theories and from there examines what Aleister Crowley and other magicians have written. We'll attempt to show how *anyone*, with the proper knowledge, can bring invisible beings through a Ouija board from the far reaches of other dimensions into our own world.

Magicians have long known that the triangular shape of the planchette is such a unique magickal and archetypal symbol that it automatically acts as an invisible doorway. When any unsuspecting person places their hands on the triangle and asks, "Is Someone there?" it enacts a simplistic but nevertheless *magical command* for the closest astral entity to be summoned through the portal.

We've all heard horror stories of how this has accidentally occurred through the board: it is legendary for causing such tragedies as obsessions, possession, or the unleashing of terrifying poltergeists and hauntings. These problems have occurred through the *misuse* of the board—that is the key. What the average person fails to realize is that these unsuccessful ventures prove beyond a shred of doubt that the board is capable of bridging the invisible world with our own, but it must be done correctly. You will be taught how to cast open the invisible gates, and you'll learn about the dark secrets which have been only whispered behind closed doors for centuries.

— J. Edward Cornelius

CHAPTER ONE

*"A few simple instructions are all that is necessary, and I shall be
pleased to give these, free of charge, to any one."*

—ALEISTER CROWLEY ON THE OUIJA BOARD

Although simply titled, this book is about far more than
the Ouija board, one of the most underappreciated
ceremonial implements of modern times. Like astrology, Tarot cards, crystal gazing and other forms of magickal
techniques and paraphernalia that have made their way into
mainstream society, the talking board has been reduced to
little more than toy status. In some ways we have to thank the
spiritualists' movement of the nineteenth century for this folly.
They've degraded this and many other sacred mysteries in their
often fraudulent quest to communicate with the deceased or
the spirit world. It has been almost impossible for the board to
shake the negative stigma that it works only in the lower astral
plane or with subconscious meanderings. And because of this
blemish, many ceremonial magicians refuse to acknowledge
the possibility of using the board in a ritual setting, fearing
ridicule by their peers if it became known that they were using
a talking board.

Although magicians like to claim that they approach
all subjects of magick from a scientific point of view, many
would rather perform safer rituals of a subjective nature,

which, although important in their own right, give little evidence outside the mind of the beholder that anything has really happened. Rarely is any *objective* magick undertaken in which we hear about a magician invoking an entity from another realm into ours. The idea of communicating with demons, angels or even elementals and a whole host of other "little folk" is mythic at best in the minds of most. Many believe these entities don't exist and will argue that they are merely allegorical.

However, history has shown that some magicians have dared to step outside this belief structure and have actually communicated with invisible entities. Aleister Edward Crowley (1875–1947) knew that human sexual polarity or magnetism could be utilized in such a way that two individuals working together could open a doorway into these subtle realms. Although this book is not meant to be a treatise on western Tantra, or sex magick, I'd like to point out that Crowley used both women and men in roles that enabled him to lift the veils and draw down invisible entities. His first wife, Rose Edith Kelly, put Crowley in contact with an entity known as Aiwass. Other examples are Mary d'Este Sturges, who put him in touch with Abuldiz; Soror Roddie Minor allowed Crowley to communicate with the spirit Amalantrah; and the poet Victor Neuberg helped Crowley work with the Enochian Angels. With his teachings, the art of ceremonial magick and the talking board can merge because the same principles of polarity are applied in both cases. Two people working together can open a doorway.

Aleister Crowley took the practice of magick into depths few individuals could ever imagine; many believe he is indisputably the greatest of all authorities on the subject. His writings provide us with a unique glimpse into the nature of the talking board's capability as a ritualistic implement, something that many people seem to ignore. In fact, Crowley *advocated its use*. If it were only a parlor game, would the likes of the Great Beast have given this implement any consideration at all?

Grady Louis McMurtry (1918–1985) was the previous world leader of Aleister Crowley's infamous fraternity known as Ordo Templi Orientis. He had been one of Crowley's students since the early '40s and had met the Great Beast numerous times while serving as a young Army officer during World War II. I met Grady in 1977, and he spent time at my house in Connecticut on several occasions. During one of our many talks on magick, the conversation drifted into spiritism and ghost-hunting. On this subject we shared common stories and good laughs; however, one topic made Grady extremely serious. When I mentioned the Ouija board to ask his opinion on its use, without hesitation he stressed strongly that it was his and Crowley's belief that it was not a toy to be played with lightly, and that the average person walks on dangerous ground when using the board. In fact, he said, knowing what he does about the board, he'd never use it casually. This bewildered me while piquing my curiosity.

He obliged me with a lengthy discourse, the gist of which was that a talking board utilizes the same angelic principles practiced by the Elizabethan magician John Dee (1527–1608). The board could be used to summon Enochian or lower elemental forces, which, as any true magician will attest, can be very dangerous if left unchecked. Grady further pointed out that John Dee looked *into* the invisible realms, known as Aethyrs, through the use of a crystal ball. Here the angels appeared and communicated their messages by pointing to one letter at a time on huge boards of letters.

The same principle, he said, holds true for the talking board, but, instead of going within the realm of the angels, we bring the entities out into our world to communicate in the same fashion, allowing them to move the triangle from one letter to another to spell out messages. Enochian magick is so unique that it comes with a warning that no one should dabble in its affairs unless extremely well-versed in the subject. Even non-believers who have attempted experiments have had strange if not dangerous things happen to them. Like the Ouija board, it doesn't matter whether you believe in the system or not; it simply works.

However, intellectually what many individuals achieve through their Enochian workings is frighteningly similar to what is usually obtained when using the board as a parlor game. Grady said it best, and I have come to agree with him, that the ultimate secret when beginning to use the board is not to simply ask "Is someone there?" You must know exactly who is being summoned and from where. You do not want to blindly open a doorway into the lower astral plane. Otherwise, what one obtains through a Ouija board, if not from a lower elemental, is little more than a lucid window whereby uncontrolled imagery from the subconscious mind is allowed to ramble forth, filtering through into reality. Magickal success with a Ouija board can only be achieved if it is used in conjunction with ritualistic and ceremonial techniques of High Magick. This is where the teachings of Aleister Crowley come into the picture.

In some ways I agree with those researchers who have wondered whether or not the board is safe for the average person to use; like Grady, I too believe that it is probably one of the most dangerous devices ever placed in the hands of humanity. It easily opens the doorway to an invisible world, allowing individuals to immerse themselves into realms beyond their wildest fantasies by merely laying their hands upon an instrument called the planchette, or pointer. The Ouija board is well known for causing such tragedies as obsessions and possessions, hauntings, or the unleashing of terrifying poltergeists. It is an instant portal into the lower astral plane. Yet these types of manifestations *prove beyond a shred of a doubt* that the board is capable of bridging the invisible world with our own.

Magicians have long known that many of the problems with the board have occurred through its *misuse*. But if the average person on the street can use the board and accidentally unleash something from the lower astral, which can terrorize their home in the form of a poltergeist, then why couldn't one well-versed in the magickal arts use the board more effectively to communicate with the invisible realms? After all, the board is simply an implement that acts as a doorway. The ability to utilize the board correctly is determined by one's magickal and spiritual training.

The most hardened critics who speak out against using the board may feel otherwise. To them the question is simply, "How do we stop the unearthly or demonic manifestations from occurring?" The magician, on the other hand, should be asking, "How do we open the portal *correctly* and control those invisible beings that are normally attracted to the Ouija board like a moth to the light?" Some uncontrolled antics of these invisible mischief-makers are legendary. The Ouija board is not a toy, but instead of shuffling the board into a closet, or burying it in "about a foot and a half of earth" and then sprinkling it with holy water[1] as those self-professed demonologists or the exorcist team of Ed and Lorraine Warren would have you do, it would be better to attempt a serious understanding of its mechanics.

Some may wonder why I quote Ed and Lorraine Warren, considering that their reputation amongst occultists is that of Christian fearmongers who have done little more than spread paranoia about the Ouija board rather than try to understand its mysteries. This couple claims to have investigated nearly 8000 cases of ghosts, apparitions and demons, as well as possessed people, places and things. They have been doing this for decades; widely lecturing and writing books on their experiences, they have waged a personal war against what they feel are diabolical forces of demonic possession. They believe that the Ouija board has been responsible for some of the tragedies that they have witnessed. For this reason alone I feel that some of their highly publicized comments need addressing.

After reading their paperback biography *The Demonologist*,[2] I felt that I had immersed myself into the Dark Ages as the book was trying to scare me with religious evils. I could only think of

Aleister Crowley who, after reading Arthur Edward Waite's *The Book of Black Magic,* stated a piece of profound wisdom: "Ah! Mr.Waite, the world of Magic is a mirror, wherein who sees muck is muck!"[3]

I am not saying that the Warrens' fear is not well-founded, or that the board could not be problematic and should not be used by children unless carefully supervised, but these two take any danger regarding the Ouija board to religious extremes. When Ed Warren appeared on the *Coast to Coast A.M.* radio show in October of 1999, he said, "... don't use Ouija Boards, don't hold seances, don't go into any kind of occult practices. If you want to learn about the supernatural, go to church." But if one person after another disappears in shark-infested waters, should we advocate that humanity never swims again and that it must run off to the Church for sanctity and information on fish? I believe the Church is often too blinded by the premise of good and evil, categorizing everything as either black or white, and claiming things to be evil simply through ignorance.

I do not agree with the Warrens' assessment of the Ouija board, but that one should learn the subtle nature of the board and the laws which govern the inner terrain, rather than burying the board in the backyard under a foot and a half of earth. The Warrens believe "The Ouija board has proven to be a notorious passkey to terror,"[4] reflecting the standard folklore regarding the Ouija board. For instance, it is the general belief that if you dispose of the board improperly then the spirits you've summoned will come back to haunt you. Many sources claim that you should break the board into seven pieces and put the remnants into a deep hole, then you must say a prayer over it and sprinkle it with Holy Water before burying the board. I have also read that if you burn the board it might scream, and those who have heard the Ouija scream have all died within thirty-six hours.

Some other typical myths and superstitions regarding the Ouija are that if the planchette goes from one corner to the next, hitting all four, it implies that you have contacted an evil spirit, and if the planchette falls off the board while you're playing, the spirit will get loose. Another way to tell if you have an evil spirit is if the planchette repeatedly makes a figure eight. However, if a silver coin is placed upon the board from the start, then no evil spirit can come through. All these, of course, are pure balderdash. There have been some cases that ended tragically after an individual began using the Ouija board, but these are rare considering the thousands of uneventful excursions daily.

As further evidence that the board is dangerous, the Warrens point out that the original story behind *The Exorcist,* written by William Peter Blatty in 1971,[5] is completely true and it occurred when a young boy (not a girl) began "using a Ouija Board!"[6] They are correct; *The Exorcist* is based on a real incident. It began in January of 1949, when a young boy was given a Ouija board as a gift by an aunt who had a strong interest in the occult and spiritism. She was dying of multiple sclerosis, and, being extremely close to the boy, gave him the board as a means to keep in touch with her after death. She died later that month on January 26th, 1949. Unfortunately, instead of reaching his aunt he opened a portal and allowed an entity to manifest that reportedly invaded his body. At the time this story broke, both *The Evening Star* and *The Washington Post* ran articles about this young boy's possession. The headlines of the *Post* on August 20th, 1949 told the story: "Priest Frees Mt. Rainer (Md.) Boy Reported Held in Devil's Grip."

It serves no purpose to go into all the gruesome details, but it is well known that William Blatty, a student at Georgetown University at the time, read these stories in the paper and years later based his book upon them. Blatty himself has even stated that "*The Exorcist* is, of course, based on an actual case that is factual, documented"[7] and he has referred to this incident. The Ouija board was involved in the original event that allowed an entity to cross over between the planes and possess a young boy. However, we should not think of this as baneful, but as a lesson in learning about the board's capability: it can draw down entities, plain and simple.

The movie *The Exorcist* was released the day after Christmas, December 26th, 1973. In addition to being one of the most horrifying movies ever made, it was probably the single most devastating piece of propaganda that gave the Ouija board its notoriety as being evil. Even the priest Father John J. Nicola, who acted as technical advisor to the movie, is quoted as saying, "I don't think I would release the film to the general public if it were up to me because of the dangers of hysteria."[8]

In the movie and the book, the Ouija board is portrayed rather graphically as the passkey. At the beginning an eleven-year-old girl named Regan MacNeil is asked if she was "playin' with the Board?" Regan simply replies "Yep." It is during this conversation that one learns that she is communicating with an entity calling itself Captain Howdy. When asked why the entity chose this moniker, Regan casually explains "'Cause that's his name, of course."[9] What wasn't really obvious in the movie was that the name was carefully chosen by the invisible intruder to mimic Regan's father, whose name was Howard. The entity knew that Regan deeply missed her father after her parents' divorce, and used a twisted version of her father's name to gain Regan's unconscious trust. In time we learn that this entity is nothing less than the epitome of pure evil and through the Ouija board he gains access into our world. The end result is the possession of young Regan with an exorcist being called in to rid the body of the demon.

Unfortunately, the entire gist of the movie seems to imply that if one plays with the Ouija board you'll become possessed, spit pea-green soup, learn fascinating sexual tricks with a cross, and speak foully to whomever you want, priest and mother alike. After it was released, people started to believe that if they played with a Ouija board they would suffer the same fate as poor little Regan and become possessed by Pazuzu or some other ill-favored demon. Although the Most Rev. Michael Ramsey, Archbishop of Canterbury, responded that "I believe there is genuine demonic possession and genuine exorcism but that which is portrayed in the movie is largely superstitious, morbid, fiddlesticks and a sign of religious immaturity,"[11] *The Exorcist* is most likely the single greatest reason why many people got rid of their Ouija boards.

The Exorcist is not the first movie to portray a Ouija board as an evil doorway. In 1920 Max Fleischer released a cartoon called *Ouija Board, Koko the Clown*. It is very short but carries the distinction of being the very first film ever to feature the board. Since then, there have been dozens: for instance, the classic 1960s movie *Thirteen Ghosts* has a great Ouija board scene where the ghost tells the family that it was going to kill one of them. And there was the third in the Amityville series, *Amityville 3-D* (1983). It was one of Meg Ryan's first films, and probably one she'd like to forget. (Obviously she hadn't seen the first two movies; otherwise, she would have known the answer to her question when she asked the board, "Is there anyone in this room who is in real danger?") Even the Warrens, who had investigated the house at Amityville, would have found this movie tragic and pointless.

The board also played a key role in *The Devil's Gift* (1984). The plot is simple: a mother looking for a birthday gift for her son finds a cute little cymbal-playing monkey in a second-hand store and buys it. What she doesn't know is that an evil spirit had been conjured through a Ouija board and now resides in this little toy which, when angry, becomes a bad monkey. Another movie is *Spookies* (1985). With a redundant plot like an old mansion, a group of kids who all deserve to die and a Ouija board being found in a closet, is there any wonder of the outcome? There is also the classic *Witchboard* series of movies that portrays the board as a means of conjuring evil spirits.

Many movies have used the board to explain how an evil entity was able to manifest and cause havoc in our world.

However, not all portray it as an evil implement: closer to the truth of a positive application of a Ouija board is seen in the movie *Awakenings* (1990). Here a doctor (Robin Williams) is experimenting with catatonic patients. While using a Ouija board with one of his non-responsive patients (Robert De Niro), he discovers that the man is actually functioning at a deep subconscious level.

As for the standard toy-like Ouija board, it has been distributed quietly for years without fanfare, yet it is beginning to enjoy a modest comeback with a new generation of people who want to dabble in its affairs. You can find the Ouija board displayed in toy stores across the country and advertised in gift magazines recommended for children as a means of entertainment. One advertisement humorously claims, "The Ouija Board is back and it's smarter than ever!" Another ad asks, "Remember when scaring the heck out of yourself was easy and fun?" There is even a Ouija Board mouse pad: "Stuck for an answer? If your computer can't tell you, try consulting 'the oracle'!"

The Ouija is once again coming out of the closet and the time is ripe for understanding the Truth behind the magickal mechanism that makes the triangle move. The most difficult thing will be to convince the public that the Ouija board is not a child's toy or a passkey to evil spirits. The talking board is simply a magickal instrument that can be used correctly or incorrectly. There is the possibility of serious problems occurring if one is not careful or well trained in the Arts, but it is our belief that one should not wallow in the negative stigmas regarding the Ouija board any more than discussing the problems, both practical and magickal, which are inherent in any topic. If you believe in the fears that the board is the archetype of pure evil, you'll miss out on the wealth of rewards that can be achieved through its use. With this book we shall discuss how to achieve positive results through the board and avoid the pitfalls normally attributed to it.

CHAPTER TWO

*"Believe in the Ouija board? I should say not.
I'm not a spiritist. I'm a Presbyterian."*

—WILLIAM FULD

At this stage, one might be asking what makes such a simple object act as a doorway between worlds—after all, it's only plastic and wood? You might also be wondering where the Ouija board originally came from, who invented it and how does it really work? Is it an ancient or modern invention? The answers are usually both contradictory and controversial because there is nothing more perplexing than the simplicity of how a Ouija board works, and although many have opinions, no one really knows its origin.

The Ouija board as we know it today originated around 1890. However, communicating with spirits and the Gods has occurred in every country since ancient times. Devices or methods similar to the talking board were used, long before the birth of Confucius, by the Chinese in order to communicate with their ancestors. Similar methods were and still are used in the En Chu Temples in Taiwan. Here, mediums known as *chi shengs* work either alone or in pairs. They sit before a large tray of white sand and in their hands they hold a V-shaped writing tool. After appropriate prayers, their hands begin to shake and the implement begins writing out messages in the sand.

In Greece, circa 540 B.C., the philosopher Pythagoras was said to use a special talking table on wheels. With hands placed upon the table it would move toward different signs and symbols. Pythagoras, or his pupil Philolaus, would then interpret the message to the waiting audience as being divine revelations supposedly from an unseen world. Some authors have even speculated the signs were merely the Greek alphabet. In ancient Rome we also find references to spirit boards. Some tribes of the American Indians used a spirit board, covered with strange symbols, which they called a *squdilatc*. The Ouija design itself may be relatively modern but the principle behind its use has been around ever since man first had a thirst to converse with the spirit world.

The Greeks had numerous unique ways of communicating with the realm of the spirits, although many of their methods are only speculation and it is often impossible to trace the origins of the stories that have come down to us. The Delphi oracles are one of the classic unsolved mysteries of the ancient world: although Greek historians have mentioned the oracles throughout the centuries, very little of the actual techniques that the priestesses employed were ever committed to paper. We know that the priestesses of Delphi were called the Pythia and were usually women over fifty, and rarely were there more than three of them at any given time. Pythia was a title taken from Pytho, the giant serpent that was slain by the god Apollo. Their temple was built over a large. circular, volcanic chasm on the southern slopes of Mount Parnassus in which it was believed Apollo had thrown the body of the slain Pytho.

History informs us that at the Temple of Delphi a large tripod was positioned over this chasm in a room known as the Adyton. The tripod was symbolic of the three phases of time ruled by Apollo: the past, present and the future. The tripod not only created the sacred Pythagorean symbol of the tetrahedron, but its base mimicked the magician's Magickal Triangle wherein entities are summoned and bound. In the center of the tripod was said to hang a pendulum suspended by a long chain, although other historians have claimed that it was a small boiling pot of herbs. The priestess, or Pythiaon, would sit atop the tripod on a special chair. After making the appropriate animal sacrifice in the flames of the basin, Pythia would breathe in the rising smoke, which the Greeks believed to be inhabited by the oracles. At this point Pythia would become possessed and enter into a trance state. Some believe that her words became divine. Other historians point out that they were often incoherent gibberish and that the greater mystery may have lain in the swinging pendulum. Some have speculated that the gods would move it back and forth, answering the question of those who wished to consult the oracle with either yes or no. The description of the method that the Delphi oracles applied varies widely depending upon the Greek scholar or historical source. Still, the Greek historian Strabo (63 B.C.–21 A.D.), who wrote of Delphi, has stated, "of all oracles in the world it had a reputation of being most truthful."

We know that small tripods and pendulums were widely used as a means of divination throughout ancient Greece. This particular type of communication carries the name which some believe goes as far back as Delphi. It is known as Dactylomancy. This term is derived from the fact that the intent behind the method of a pendulum was to communicate with the invisible entities or oracles called Dactyls. These oracles acted as go-betweens for mortals and Gods. The word Delphi comes from the Greek *delphos*, meaning womb, and legend has it that the Dactyls were born at Delphi. They came to birth when the sky goddess Rhea laid her fingers upon the earth and from each fingertip sprang forth an invisible child, five girls and five boys, whose destiny was to protect young Zeus from Kronos, his father. Zeus of course survived, and in turn became the father of Apollo, whose temple stands at Delphi.

Like many astral or invisible beings, the Dactyls were armed with shield and sword, often casting spells both good and evil upon mankind at the request of those who summoned them. Some have even interpreted this ancient myth of Rhea to represent a type of practice that is symbolically linked with the talking boards. After all, when using a Ouija board, you lay their hands on the triangle and from your fingertips spring forth invisible children who are willing to communicate and assist in any way they can. As with many myths, this one has subtly woven itself into present-day society. The Greek word for finger is *dactyl*. Fingers have always been a powerful tool and have played an important role in many different mythologies, religions and in magick itself. Fingers are part of the hand, which Aleister Crowley refers to as the *magickal instrument par excellence*.

With the passage of time the sacred art of Dactylomancy has wrongly been reduced to imply any form of divination where pendulums or rings are used. One of the earliest recorded instances of divination by pendulum occurred in the fourth century. During this period, the Byzantine historian Ammianus Marcellinus tells how Fidustius, Patricius, and Hilarius were arrested for trying to divine the name of the Emperor who would succeed Valens (364–378 A.D.) by use of a pendulum. According to the story, they admitted to using a small round dish which had the alphabet painted around the rim. They suspended the pendulum in the middle of this dish, and when it began to move it spelled out the name of the great general Theodosius. Emperor Valens upon hearing this news was so outraged that he had the unsuspecting Theodosius immediately killed. However, the Gods are rarely wrong. What wasn't foreseen was that Theodosius' son, also named Theodosius, would become the next emperor upon the death of Valens.

The use of pendulums was widespread in the ancient world. Even up into the last century it was a standard practice for women to use their wedding rings attached to a string that they would suspend near a glass. This method was similar to the ancient Roman technique. When a question was asked, the ring would begin to swing. If it struck the glass it implied a yes or no answer. The same results are achieved by suspending the pendulum between cards on which were written yes and no. A far more complicated version based upon this theme emerged with the pendulum suspended in the middle of a circle, around which the letters of the alphabet were laid out on individual cards, along with a yes and no card. When a question was asked, the pendulum would begin to swing toward one letter after another, slowly spelling out words.

Although this art was still called Dactylomancy during this early period of spiritism, the Dactyls were pushed aside, becoming little more than a Greek myth. The invisible kingdoms were becoming Christianized, bathed in either good or evil. Everything had to be black or white. Spiritists had to be careful when referring to the source behind their communications: asking for advice from the deceased was tolerated at best, while claiming to communicate with anything else was considered demonic and was often attacked by society. Myths like the Dactyls were seen as an imaginary or fictitious metaphor simply used to teach by example. The idea that within these myths is concealed greater truths was tragically ignored.

As for the triangle used with the talking boards, this appeared in the last century but it had absolutely no connection to Dactylomancy. It was often referred to as the "traveler" by many psychic researchers of the period, and like many implements it was born out of the age of spiritism with its table-rapping and spirit communications. Once introduced, spirit communications spread like wildfire. It seemed that every major city had its share of mediums and spiritists. The methods used in the attempts to communicate with a vast array of spiritual beings were so varied that they can only be summed up as creative.

One such method widely used in the last century was known as automatism. No one really knows how or where automatic writing slipped into the picture, but this technique implies that an individual could be writing without any conscious awareness of his or her actions. While in a trance state, a pencil was placed between a medium's fingers and a piece of paper was slipped under their hand. Often the individual would begin scribbling strange notes, weird drawings or bizarre messages, usually in a handwriting totally different than that used by the person's conscious self, and sometimes even in a foreign language. It was generally believed that these messages came directly from a spirit who was guiding the hand of the medium but, in all honesty, most of what was achieved was simply unrecognizable scribbling.

Legend has it that an important development in automatism occurred in 1853. A French spiritualist named M. Planchette designed a unique device that was the original forerunner of the triangle used with our modern Ouija board. His triangle, or table as it's often called, was heart-shaped and made of wood. It had two small legs resting on tiny-wheeled casters to enable it to move easily, while the third leg in the front was a wooden pencil. The point was pushed downward through a tiny outlet lined with rubber to hold the pencil firmly in place. A person would rest their hand on top of this device before slipping into a trance. When the table moved, it spelled out the message on a piece of paper. To this day the pointer, or triangle, of a Ouija is often referred to as the planchet or planchette, named after its original inventor.

Others disagree with this piece of history, claiming that it was an earlier American spiritist named Thomas Welton who was the real inventor of the triangular device. It seems that Welton's fascination for crystal gazing in the 1850s was well-renowned. In fact, he even published a pamphlet titled *The Planchette* to express that he and not Planchette had created this device. Whether true or not, his claims have been all but ignored in history. Today it's generally believed that Planchette was the real inventor. Another controversial opinion on this piece of historical rhetoric suggests that M. Planchette never existed: no hardcore evidence has ever surfaced to substantiate his life, even though authors are always writing about him as if he was a real person who had lived in France. Planchette is truly a mystery figure. For the sake of this argument, some historians have been quick to point out that the word "planchette" is simply a French term which could translate as "little plank" (Fr. *planche* — plank, board) which is, after all, what a planchette is. This is probably closer to the truth.

The design behind the modern talking board is equally webbed in historical myths, all very contradictory depending upon whom you're reading. The nineteenth century was an age when anyone could spin a yarn, create a fable and tell the "truth" as they seemingly saw it. Plagiarism was running wild and history was being written, rewritten and often rewritten again by every individual who professed that they alone had created a device that people could use in order to communicate with the spirit world. If anyone has ever wondered why spiritists have gotten a bad reputation, they need only study the history of this period: many individuals who practiced Spiritism conducted themselves in an unscrupulous, if not shyster-like, manner bordering on stage-show antics. They often sold their trade from town to town as if it were a carnival sideshow. This makes writing an accurate history of the period of spiritualism almost impossible.

We do know that whoever came up with the "original" idea of the talking board borrowed pieces from many of the spiritualistic gadgets of their day. Their variation on Planchette's device was to simply remove the pencil, thus allowing the triangle to point to a desired letter that had been painted upon a rectangular wooden board, one letter at a time, until a message was achieved. With this, two important methods of the period merged: the planchette and the idea of painting the alphabet on a separate board, which was probably taken from the earlier dial-plates machines.

The oldest written record of dial-plates is found in Allan Kardec's book *Le Livre des Mediums*, published in 1861. His real name was Hippolyte Leon Denizard Rivail (1804–1869) and he was considered by some to be the founder of French spiritism. He wrote the classic handbook titled *The Book of Spirits* that became the standard work on spiritualistic doctrine. The dial-plates themselves were a unique and cumbersome device. Most were circular boards with the alphabet painted either around the top or bottom part of the perimeter. We are not so concerned with those designs that required just one person to move the dial-plate, but are more interested in those dial-plates that required the use of two individuals. It is believed that they are the forerunner of the present-day design of the Ouija board.

These particular dial-plates had a long T-shaped bar balanced across the middle of an upright circular board. Two people held on to either side of the T-bar. The part that extended downward was the pointer. When the T-bar began to rock, it moved the pointer to different letters which had been painted around the bottom of the board. The innovation of making the pointer move by utilizing two people is a remarkable piece of genius. The means to achieve movement without conscious interference had been known for a while: many reputable individuals of that period in France had been experimenting with the concept that objects of extraordinary weight could be lifted and transported by the magnetic polarity inherently found in the Astral Light. This is something which spiritists did not discover or invent, but simply incorporated into their methods.

This ability to move objects had been used very successfully with table-tapping. This is where two or more people place their hands palm downward on a small wooden table, fingers outstretched to touch the person's fingers on either side, thus forming an unbroken circle. A question was then asked and the table would usually begin to rock, shake or gently move across the floor. What was unique about this concept is that it confirmed that two or more people with no apparent psychic ability could move an object simply by placing their fingers upon it. Of course, like many practices, some spiritists degraded this art in order to make money—if a client was unable to move the table then the medium, fearing the loss of their bread and butter, assisted in a fraudulent manner by trickery.

Unfortunately, once one medium had been caught cheating, society blindly began to believe that *all* spiritists were frauds. Newspapers often looked for such sensational stories to sell their pulp, and gleefully spread diatribes about swindlers; there was very little rebuttal of a positive nature offered in the spiritists' defense. The sheer weight of bad publicity spelled the beginning of the end for the movement as a whole. The time was ripe for the emergence of the Ouija board. If the art was going to survive, it had to be taken away from the hands of the frauds and placed in the hands of humanity as a whole. Although the boards were publicly sold, the practice went behind closed doors and beyond the prying eyes of journalists and debunkers.

The earliest possible facts upon which historians can agree about the origins of the "Ouija" as we know it today center around E.C. Reiche, a coffin maker in Chestertown, Maryland. It is generally believed that he had a strong interest in spiritism and table-tapping due to his unique trade. He wanted to create a simple means to communicate with the deceased more for personal reasons rather than something for the public. Initially he "noticed sympathetically that a large table was a heavy thing for a frail spirit to juggle about [so] he devised a little table."[1] When he teamed up with his two friends, Elijah J. Bond and Charles Kennard, they put their heads together and the three of them created the final design for the talking board. However, no written records survive which allow these facts to be easily verified. At this point we can only speculate as to what might have inspired these three gentlemen or from where their original design might have come.

Of these three, E.C. Reiche seems to quietly disappear into history and is all but forgotten. Charles Kennard, on the other hand, opened the first company to manufacture the talking boards for the public in 1890. Other historians claim it was Elijah J. Bond who started the company, but its original name was the Kennard Novelty Company. Some believe both gentlemen simply worked together on this project and, later, each told the story as if they had founded the business. To add to the confusion, although the business was called the Kennard Novelty Company, the patent for the talking board filed in 1891 was in Elijah Bond's name.

Regardless of who started the company, prior to these two gentlemen, communing with the spirit world had been something reserved almost exclusively by mediumistic people who had special spiritualistic tools or implements at their disposal. With the emergence of Kennard's Ouija board this was no longer the case. Spirit communication was being sold openly to the general public, to anyone who had $1.50 to buy a board, much to the dismay of psychics and mediums. The gates to the invisible world were thrown wide open and have been so ever since. Kennard's original advertisement in a local paper read: "Ouija. A Wonderful Talking Board. Interesting and mysterious; surpasses in its results, second sight, mind reading, clairvoyance; will give intelligent answers to any question. Proven at patent office before patent was allowed."

Although impossible to confirm, it is generally believed that while Kennard was using a talking board, a spirit told him the correct name for his new device. It was *Ouija*. The spirit explained that this was an ancient Egyptian word meaning "Good Luck." Some historians disagree, claiming that it was E.C. Reiche who had been working the board at the time when the name came through; others have suggested the confusion is due to the fact that both gentlemen may have been working the board together. Typical to the period, when recounting what was obtained, each told the story as if he and he alone were present. Of course, modern Egyptologists are quick to point out that no such word exists in the Egyptian language, as far as they know. Nonetheless, this was how the name Ouija was originally obtained and it has stuck ever since.

The company ran fairly smoothly for Kennard in the beginning, but had he been using the board for advice he would have foreseen trouble. In early 1892 there was a hostile takeover of his company by two of his financial backers, Isaac and William Fuld. The latter had previously been the foreman of his company. In need of money, Kennard was forced to sell the business. The Fuld brothers then decided to file for another patent as the new owners, and registered such on July 19th, 1892. The patent was put in only William's name, which would later prove problematic for Isaac.

The two brothers immediately changed the name of their new company to the Ouija Novelty Company. William was said to have been an interesting and imaginative character who not only began to reinvent the history of the board, with himself as its inventor, but he also changed the story of what the word "Ouija" actually means. The tale that it was an Egyptian word obtained through the board fell by the wayside. In fostering a new mythos, William never denied that the board named itself, but changed the meaning behind the term Ouija. He started claiming that it was two different words put together, both of which mean "yes." One is French (Oui) and the other German, or Ja. This definition as a "yes-yes" board is what most people believe the word Ouija means.

As with the previous business, there were dark clouds on the horizon for this company as well. It was as if a curse had been evoked upon anyone who dared to make a profit off the spirits. Besides the fierce competition from numerous companies flooding the market with imitation talking boards, Isaac and William were having personal difficulties. This came to a head when Isaac was accused of bookkeeping shenanigans by William, who subsequently fired him. William then changed the name of the company to the Baltimore Talking Board Company. He also made a unique change in the design of the planchette in 1910, which is still used today: he added a circular window to improve the viewing of the letters. Isaac went on to create his own talking board company called Oriole. His boards were almost an exact duplicate of the original design created by Kennard, except with Kennard's name removed and replaced with the name Oriole. Each board had a sticker on the back that read the Southern Toy Company.

Obviously, due to the personal animosity between the brothers, their companies were destined for further confrontation. This ended with both brothers in court arguing as to who should be credited with the original design on the patent. The future of both companies lay in the balance. Although the family gave their nod toward Isaac, it was William who ended up recognized by the courts as the board's creator. Sadly, Charles Kennard's earlier patent design was not even brought into the picture.

A reporter from *The Literary Digest* at the time voiced surprise over the fact that the Fuld brothers were fighting in court over who had created the original idea, commenting, "Why don't they ask the ouija itself regarding the division of the spoils? Wouldn't the Greeks have consulted the Delphic oracle if they had fallen into a dispute about said oracle?"[2] To this, William Fuld responded, "Believe in the Ouija board? I should say not. I'm not a spiritist. I'm a Presbyterian."[3] The reporter replies, "So there you are, ouija fans, Mr. Fuld makes the only ouija, patented in the United States and Canada and trade-marked all over the world, but he wouldn't trust it with so much as a question about the weather."[4]

However, many people didn't believe in William Fuld's public denial and felt that he had been secretly using the board behind closed doors, especially considering that in the early 1920s it became known that he decided to expand the company and build a new building on the advice given to him through one of his own talking boards. A reporter, quick to pick up on this story, asked William whether or not he had been continuously consulting his Ouija board. He simply replied, "Nope. I built this factory on Ouija's advice, but I haven't consulted the board since then."[5] As to why he stopped playing the board, he replied that since building the company everything was "moving along so well I didn't want to start anything"[6] or to stir anything up. Although he no longer sought the advice of his talking board, or so he claimed, the company remained extremely successful for many years.

Then tragedy struck. In February of 1927 the headlines in the local paper read, "Wm. Fuld is Killed in Fall from Roof."[7] It seems William accidentally fell off the roof of his Baltimore company and plunged three stories to his death. He was only 54. Of course there were immediate rumors circulating of a suicide, since the business had supposedly fallen on hard times. Others who were actually present disagreed, claiming that William was supervising the assembly of a new flagpole when the support post he was leaning against gave way. They said he simply fell backwards off the roof. Still, the suicide stories persist to this day. As for Isaac, he died twelve years later on November 18th, 1939 at the age of 74, never getting the credit some believe he deserved.

After William's death the company was taken over by two of his sons, William and Hubert. At first, everything ran very smoothly but they began having difficulties supplying the quantity needed for the stores; some believe they simply wanted out of the business. Knowing this, the Parker Brothers approached the family in 1966 and found them receptive to the idea of another family-owned firm taking over as sole producer of the "mystifying oracle." An article appeared in *The New York Times* that mentioned the sale of the company, titled "Monopoly on Ouija."[8] It went on to say, "Parker Brothers, Inc, the Salem, Mass., maker of games such as Monopoly, announced yesterday that it had acquired full ownership of William Fuld, Inc. ... This would ordinarily be a routine acquisition except that the Fuld group is owner of the registered United States trademark 'Ouija.'" Parker Brothers had purchased the copyright and to this day still produces the same board under the registered trademarks of "Ouija Board" and "Mystifying Oracle." For a brief period the Ouija Board even outsold Monopoly!

If you were to purchase the game today you'd find absolutely no information within the box except a piece of paper, about the size of a small filing card, which tells you how to mount the felt feet onto the triangle. At one time there was a booklet enclosed, or so I remembered as a child in the early '60s when my family owned a Ouija. I recently purchased the board to obtain this booklet but discovered no such thing in the box. When I tried to obtain a copy from Parker Brothers I was kindly told "The booklet that was included in the game is no longer available,"[9] end of subject. The only information on the Ouija is now found on the back of the box itself, where it simply states that "Whether you call it Wee-Gee ... or Wee-Ja ... the OUIJA board spells fun!" There is a brief paragraph on how to make the "plastic message indicator" move, which is their name for the planchette. The blurb on the box ends by stating, "What you do with the information it reveals is between you—and the Mystifying Oracle! OUIJA ... is only a game ... isn't it?"[10] Regardless of such an alluring comment, the board is sold as if it were a child's game that anyone can play without the slightest precautions.

Because of its toy status, any mention of the Ouija board becomes extremely complicated, if not controversial. It all boils down to whether one believes it's a game or a means of communicating with entities from the other side, which was actually argued in a court of law. In 1920 the Baltimore Ouija Company fought hard against paying taxes on the grounds that the Ouija was a "scientific device" used as a means of amateur mediumship of a spiritual nature, and therefore should be exempt by its religious status. They took the Internal Revenue Service to court in order to recover a whopping $202.81 that it had protestingly paid in taxes.

However, the U.S. Court believed that although the board was unique and in a class by itself, it was still being sold in stores as a "sporting game" and was therefore taxable. The local headlines read "Nothing Occult in Ouija, Federal Court Rules. Boards are Taxable, according to Opinion Handed Down by Judge Rose."[11] The company disagreed and appealed the decision, but to no avail. The Baltimore Sun reported: "Ouija Board is Taxable, Appellate Court Says. Judge Woods, in Richmond, Hands Down Opinion Affirming Baltimore Judgement."[12] The court stated that the company "cannot pretend to be ignorant that it [Ouija] is very largely sold with the expectation that it is to be used as a means of social amusement or play and is actually so used. It is true that automatism is the basis for its use, but phenomena of psychical as well as of physical nature may be the basis for amusement and games."[13] Not to be discouraged, the Baltimore Talking Board Company filed papers on May 13th, 1922 with the U.S. Supreme Court, who refused to hear their case and sided with the lower court ruling. The headlines in Baltimore: "The Supreme Court Refuses to Say What It Thinks of Ouija."[14] The case was officially closed.

From that day forward it has become impossible to shake the stigma that a Ouija board is simply a game sold in toy stores around the world. The average person purchases the Ouija thinking it's a toy for their child, rather than something far more dangerous. Parents and children alike, without the slightest magickal training or precautions, may ask their inane questions unaware of the possibility, albeit rare, that they can accidentally drag an invisible entity, their own "Captain Howdy," through the board from the far reaches of another dimension into their world. With much regret some households with young children are subjected to all the horrors, both mental and physical, which the board might muster. As shocking as this might sound, those individuals are closer to the board's truth than they may ever wish to know. Fortunately most people have become complacent because of the board's accessibility: they don't take it seriously, and in some ways this is good. The greatest saving grace protecting humanity has been its own ignorance as to the board's proper use.

CHAPTER THREE

*"let not the reader suppose that we stopt our labor
and went at trying to win the faculty of Abrac, drawing circles,
or sooth saying, to the neglect of all kinds of business."*

— LUCY SMITH, MOTHER OF THE MORMON PROPHET

The Ouija board as it exists in its present form may not be that old, but the principles behind the use of talking boards for spirit communications have been used in various forms within secret societies and religious centers for untold years. We need to wade through all the possibilities, avoid the stigmas and approach the subject from a scientific point of view. There is little doubt that the talking board works; what should be examined further is what exactly makes the planchette move. Is it the individuals themselves, an independent entity, or both in a symbiotic relationship?

In recent years there are many styles of boards being manufactured, and the planchette has taken on a variety of shapes. Since the movement of the planchette utilizes the biological magnetic currents inherent in all people, every design will automatically work to some degree or another. However, the design of the planchette is important because it dictates a certain type of subtle quality being put to use. The traditional design is by far the best. It effectuates a preferred result for the ceremonial magician who knows that its shape as a magickal implement suggests the unconscious intent in an astral working. The simplicity of the planchette's shape on the standard Ouija, being somewhat heart-shaped or triangular, is often overlooked, but, like the magickal circle, the altars, robes and regalia, the triangle has a specific function.

The triangle is one side of a pyramid whose shape was used by the ancients as a tomb. The structure of a pyramid, with its apex pointing upward, projects the spirit of the deceased into the nether world. A pyramid whose apex is pointing downward is symbolic of a human womb. In this position its opening is a gateway into our world through which a specific spirit may obtain incarnation. The triangle as an image has an almost archetypal effect on our mind and especially on invisible entities like the elementals, which abound in the lower astral plane. Magicians have known for centuries that the magickal image of a triangle acts as a "between state" which is neither an entity's world or ours. In some respect it is a doorway that swings both ways. You'll find images of a triangle in the pages of almost every ancient magickal grimoire. It is within a triangle that a magician will summon a disincarnated entity in order to communicate, bind them and control them at the same time.

Israel Regardie, the author and student of Crowley, wrote that "By a programme of Evocation, however, the spirits or subconscious powers are called forth from the deep, and, giving them visible shape in the Triangle of manifestation. It is only by giving them a visible appearance, by means of the incense particles, and evoking them into the magical Triangle that the Magician is able to dominate them and to do with them as he desires."[1] Also, in the grimoire known as the *Goetia* or *The Lesser Key of Solomon,* there is an excellent example of this magickal triangle typical of which Regardie speaks: this "is the Form of the Magical Triangle, into the which Solomon did command the Evil Spirits. It is to be made at 2 feet distance from the Magical Circle and is 3 feet across. Note that this triangle is to be placed toward that quarter whereunto the Spirit belongeth.

And the base of the triangle is to be nearest unto the Circle, the apex pointing in the direction of the quarter of the Spirit."[2] The term "evil" here is webbed in the author's religious leanings as well as the times in which the book was written.

Use of the magical triangle for summoning entities has been around for centuries. The danger is not in the simplicity of the symbol itself, but rather in its misuse in effecting a gateway into the invisible world without the knowledge and ability to control that which is being summoned. Keep this in the forefront of your mind when you casually place your fingers on the planchette.

In some of the old grimoires the triangle is pictured as being laid out on a table with either a black mirror or a crystal ball on a stand in the very center. The magician stands within a specially prepared circle near the table and gazes within the crystal or mirror. Upon entering a passive trance state, the magician can perceive strange visions, images or often words. In some cases entities actually appear who guide the magician through a conversation. What can be achieved through this type of a magickal working is identical to that of a Ouija board.

Frater Achad [Charles Stansfeld Jones], one of Aleister Crowley's most ardent students, wrote a book called *Crystal Vision through Crystal Gazing*, in which he notes that in relationship to skrying (also spelled scrying) "the case of the Ouija Board applies equally to the Crystal."[3] The warnings and practices are very similar. The planchette has a clear plastic circle in its center and can be likened to a crystal. Thus, instead of using incense, a black mirror, or a crystal ball to give an entity something to reveal itself, modern man has given the spirits a tool through which to speak—the circle on the triangle. The triangular planchette is such a unique archetypal symbol that it automatically acts as a doorway when used in a specific setting designed to accomplish such results. When one asks "Is Someone there?" even when only playing a game, it becomes a simplistic but nevertheless *magical command* for the closest entity to be summoned through the portal.

Aleister Crowley stated these apparent dangers as well as the proper use of the Ouija board. His comments, published more than three years before the U.S. court decision against The Baltimore Ouija Company, lay the foundation for this book. In 1917, while living in New York, the Beast wrote an interesting article about the Ouija that was published in a newspaper called *The International*.[4] Frater Achad incorporated this article into his own *Crystal Vision through Crystal Gazing* in 1923. Crowley wrote, "Suppose a perfect stranger came into your office and proceeded to give orders to your staff. Suppose a strange woman walked into your drawing room and insisted on being hostess. You would be troubled by this. Yet, people sit down and offer the use of their brains and hands (which are, after all, more important than offices and drawing rooms) to any stray intelligence that may be wandering about. People use the Ouija Board without taking the slightest precautions."

This is so true. Many people will not give it a second thought when they give permission for an invisible entity to enter into their home through the planchette of a Ouija board. Even Ed Warren agrees with Aleister Crowley's views: "When you use the Ouija board, you give permission for any unknown spirit to communicate with you. Would you open the front door to your house and let in anybody who felt like it? Of course not."[5] However, these views are founded out of a religious fear rather than learning how to perform an experiment correctly. This is the overall problem when using the board as if it were a child's game: allowing any stranger, physical or invisible, to enter your home is half-witted. None is more important than this warning about this lack of precautions in carelessly operating the board. In this age of cyberspace, a similar warning is given to children who surf the Internet. It's just common sense— don't let strangers into your house by opening the front door, through the telephone, a computer or even a Ouija board.

What precautions can we take? How might we identify with whom we're really communicating? Crowley wrote that once an entity has been drawn through a Ouija board, the "establishment of the identity of a spirit by ordinary methods is a very difficult problem."[6] This is an accurate statement on all planes. Unless one is highly trained in magick, the identity (or rather, the type of entity) must be determined long *before* it is allowed to manifest into your surroundings, otherwise it's almost impossible to identify it as being good or malefic before it is too late. Crowley further states: "The majority of people who play at Occultism do not even worry about this. They get something, and it does not seem to matter what! Every inanity, every stupidity, every piece of rubbish, is taken not only at its face value, but at an utterly exaggerated value. The most appallingly bad poetry will pass for Shelly, if only its authentication be that of the planchette!"[7]

Certain invisible entities, which magicians call elementals, have the ability to communicate through the board and can take on the guise of whomever *we* want them to be. Since these entities have the ability to exist by mutation within the Lunar or Astral Light they are also known as shape-shifters. These entities are the easiest to summon through the board, and two people simply laying their hands on the planchette gives them access into our world through human polarity and magnetism. Their astral kingdom is comprised of a five-fold quality that on another level is mimicked by the attributes of the fingers on each hand. Crowley looks upon the hand as the "tool or instrument par excellence."[8] The reasons for such are layered, often sexual, but obvious on all planes.

Earlier we mentioned the Dactyls, the invisible entities that were brought to birth when the goddess Rhea touched her fingers upon the Earth. The Dactyls are what the witch calls a familiar, and what an unsuspecting dabbler might call a poltergeist. Others in the past have referred to these entities simply as demons or even fairies, goblins, brownies, pucks, elves, gnomes, or a whole host of other "little folk" depending upon the "type" of elemental manifesting. This is determined by the qualities of earth, fire, water or air; the fifth quality is concealed within the four. Depending upon one's beliefs the names change, but the existence of something within the invisible astral realm remains the same. However, the magician's term of "elemental" is probably closer to the truth since it acknowledges the essence of the entity before it mutates and is clothed in our personal concepts or proclivities.

Because of the elementals' nature as tricksters, some refer to them as malefic or lying spirits, even calling them demonic, which is inaccurate. Magicians are well aware that an elemental can shape-shift or assume any identity that is impressed upon it. The Moon, which rules the astral, has no light of its own. It reflects that which is impressed upon it by a Sun, or by those who live in the light of day, meaning you. Every man and every woman is a star. (*Liber AL vel Legis* I:3) It's quite simple for these entities to become Shelly, Mozart, Cleopatra, your deceased grandmother, or simply a ghost whom you think is haunting your house. Whom they become is determined by the types of questions you ask and think internally—if you want to communicate with your dead grandmother then these entities can become your deceased relative.

Still, we cannot dismiss the concept of a disincarnated entity spelling out poetry simply because Aleister Crowley might call such "appallingly bad." One must always remember Crowley's ego—he hated most poets other than himself. However, in the mundane world, if an individual gives us a bad poem we don't discourage others from trying. With the Ouija board, there have been individuals who have taken the messages they've received to the extreme, building upon previous communications one day after the next until remarkable things have been obtained. This is a clue to Ouija's success.

Another example of an individual guided by "something" is the work of Jane Roberts. She is the author of such best-selling books as *The Coming of Seth* and *The Seth Material,* both of which were obtained in 1963 after she began communicating with an entity called Seth through a Ouija board. She has a phenomenal following to this day, and her books can be found in bookstores across the world. She is not the first to achieve interesting results while using the board: on July 8th, 1913, a St. Louis housewife with very little education named Pearl Curran communicated with an entity through a Ouija board, who began by spelling out, "Many months ago I lived. Again I come. Patience Worth (is) my name." Over the next five years she obtained 29 bound volumes of material, from short stories, plays and full-length novels to simple epigrams and poems. Many were acclaimed as literary masterpieces.

There is little doubt of the remarkable relationship fostered between Pearl and an entity calling itself Patience. However, with fame came pressure and criticism. To remain amongst her newfound literary friends, Pearl began to deny that a Ouija board was responsible for producing the stories. She began claiming authorship herself. Those close to her knew otherwise; some even pointed out that she was actually too stupid to perpetrate such a fraud. Even philologists who studied her works have stated that with Curran's limited education and childlike intelligence there was no way she could have produced novels in which the majority of the words were of Anglo-Saxon derivation of a medieval nature. More perplexing to the scholars was that her novels did not contain even one word that had entered the English language after the seventeenth century. If she was a fraud, she was a damn good one.

It was during this period that Emily Hutchings, one of Pearl's friends, tried her own hand at the Ouija. She claimed to have contacted the spirit of Mark Twain who dictated to her a postmortem story. Published in 1917, it was titled *Jap Heron, A Novel Written From The Ouija Board*. Aleister Crowley reviewed this book light-heartedly in *The International*[9] under the alias of Miles, setting the tone by beginning, "Literary forgeries are sometimes interesting, but they have to be clever." He continues: "We have no doubt that the spiritualists who did it are sincere. They may think that Mark Twain wrote this book; but if so, Mark Twain has simply forgotten how to write." In fact, the book is so bad that most critics of the period questioned if Mark Twain had not left his ability to write, along with his brain, in his coffin when he died!

Crowley's greatest insight in the review is when he writes, "There appears to be a kind of painstaking imitation of the style, such as might be within the powers of one of those playful elemental spirits who love to make fun of those who invoke them without proper magical precautions," explaining that he doubts Twain wrote the book, and if he did, "It limps a thousand miles behind the very feeblest of his earthly efforts." He jokes that Mark Twain wrote a "great deal of third-rate stuff, forced humor, false sentiment, at times sheer tosh" but that "this book is a revelation of how good that bad stuff was."

Still, there are other individuals who produced interesting work through a Ouija board. The Pulitzer Prize winner James Merrill wrote a lengthy poetic work, comprising an astounding three volumes, titled *The Changing Light at Sandover*. He admitted that most of the book was co-authored by using a Ouija board in 1953—another example of remarkable things obtained through a symbiotic relationship between the board and user. The Ouija board is obviously the catalyst, the one consistent thread that these writers and others have shared. Even if you believe that all these people *only* tapped into their own creative genius, which flowed through the board, wouldn't it be important to discover how this can be focused and channeled so that your own dormant abilities can be developed? Have you ever wondered how to utilize all the information that you've forgotten throughout your incarnation which might be waiting deep in your subconscious to be processed, like stored knowledge in the mainframe of a computer?

Many of the writers I've just mentioned who began with a Ouija board later obtained the ability of automatic writing, as if to imply the development of latent powers. Contrary to popular belief, a person who uses automatic writing is not always in a deep trance or writing without any conscious awareness of their actions. Automatic writings can, in fact, be produced in the wakeful state, or rather in a semi-trance, as long as there is no interference from the conscious mind. In this manner it is similar to working a Ouija board; in both cases a person is fully conscious of any and all things that are going on around them. The secret is remaining entirely passive.

Although much of what has been achieved through automatic writing amounts to mostly unrecognizable scribbles, in some rare cases profound words and documents have been known to be channeled and spewed forth at an alarming rate through its use. Consider the book *Oahspe* that appeared in 1882: delivered through automatic writing by the self-proclaimed clairvoyant Dr. John Newbrough and hailed as the new Bible, it is 900 pages in length!

Probably the most famous occult book obtained through automatic writing is a small volume known as *Liber AL vel Legis*. This book was dictated to Aleister Crowley, while in a trance state, by an invisible entity in Cairo between noon and 1 p.m. on three successive days, April 8th, 9th and 10th, in the year 1904. The invisible author called himself Aiwass, and claimed to be "the minister of Hoor-paar-kraat"; that is, a messenger of the forces which are now ruling the Earth in the emerging Aeon of Aquarius. This new Bible lays down a very simple code of conduct for anyone who wishes to follow the philosophy behind True Will. It is: "Do what thou wilt shall be the whole of the Law," "Love is the law, love under will," and "There is no law beyond Do what thou wilt." *Thelema* is the Greek word for Will, and those who follow this Law are called Thelemites.

There are many methods whereby entities communicate with mortals. Whether we go within their realm or bring them out into ours, the result is the same: something is communicated and transpires between them and us. Even *The Book of Mormon* has its origins rooted deep in the use of ceremonial magick and angelic skrying. It is well known that Joseph Smith read the magical treatise by Francis Barrett called *The Magus* (1801). From this he learned how to use a crystal in order to obtain angelic visions. However, at first he predominantly sought buried treasure and missing items. All this information came to light when historians realized that Joseph Smith was arrested as a fraudulent "glass looker" and was found guilty in Bainbridge, New York, in 1826.

Court records state that Joseph Smith "had a certain stone which he had occasionally looked at to determine where hidden treasures in the bowels of the earth were." Smith's "peep stones," as they became known, were described by his mother Lucy in her *Biographical Sketches of Joseph Smith the Prophet* (1853) as "two smooth three-cornered diamonds set in glass, and the glasses were set in silver bows, which were connected with each other in much the same way as old fashioned spectacles."[10] Smith later called these stones his Urim and Thummim, and witnesses said they were about the size, not shape, of hen's eggs. He wore them like glasses, then covered his face with his hat to darken the background and exclude outside light. It was said that in this darkness, spiritual light was given off by the stones and visions were obtained.

In later printings of Lucy Smith's historical accounts, the description she gave of these stones was deleted. In fact, over the years the stones have undergone many marvelous description changes. This subject has forever been the bane of the Mormon Church because it implies that a form of crystal gazing was used by their prophet in acquiring their Bible.

There is another astonishing revelation made by Lucy Smith on this subject. She was concerned that after the trial everyone might think that her son Joseph and her whole family did little else but occult matters. In the preliminary draft of her book she wrote, "let not the reader suppose that we stopt our labor and went at trying to win the faculty of Abrac, drawing circles, or sooth saying, to the neglect of all kinds of business."[11] When her accounts were finally published in 1853, this paragraph, which contained the word Abrac, was conveniently omitted. However, her original drafts do survive for all to see in the historical archives of the Mormon Church. The church does not deny her statements but the mere fact that she mentions the faculty of Abrac implies she knew of, or at least heard about, secret Masonic teachings.

In Robert Hullinger's *Mormon Answer to Skepticism* (1980), he writes, "Abrac, from Abracadabra and Abraxas is a word or formula used on amulets to work magic charms. Eighteenth-century Masons were said to know how to conceal 'the way of obtaining the faculty of Abrac,' which implied that they knew how to get it."[12] The knowledge about the faculty of Abrac has been around for hundreds of years. Amongst the private papers of King Henry VI (1421–1471), in his own handwriting, is the assertion that the Masons of his period concealed "the facultye of Abrac"[12] in their private papers and teachings. The author James Hardie, as far back as 1818, confirms this in *The Free-Mason's Monitor*. So does Henry Wardin in his book *Free Masonry, Its Pretensions Exposed in Faithful Extracts of its Standard Authors,* published in 1828. Both gentlemen discuss how certain Masonic teachings lead the candidate upward to a "way of winning the faculty of Abrac."

The means by which individuals like Joseph Smith and others have obtained their interaction with the Gods are diverse and sundry. History has shown that some have used skrying or crystal gazing, while others have used divination, automatic writing and even talking boards. What many of these individuals had in common is that each took one of these seemingly simplistic arts to a level that few people could ever have foreseen unless well trained in the magickal arts.

The "faculty of Abrac" refers to an ability that allows individuals to obtain hidden knowledge or Gnosis with the spirit world and with angels. In particular it refers to specific entities that descend through our Sun, which according to the ancient Christian Gnostics is ruled by the god Abraxas. Joseph Smith's use of this formula, consciously or unconsciously, began while he was seeking buried treasure in 1823, when one of his visions told him that secret records were buried in New York. The exact location of these records was not revealed to him until four years later. These records, or golden plates, were translated by use of his "peep stones" and became known as *The Book of Mormon*. Remember, it was Joseph Smith's mother who called his peep stones "three-cornered diamonds." The magical stones whose properties most reflect the Sun are said to be diamonds. It has been speculated that Smith's peep stones might have been Herkimer diamonds, which are found in only one place in the entire world—just east of where Joseph Smith obtained his visions in Herkimer County, New York.

The Herkimer is a double-terminated quartz crystal formed in bedrock dating back half a billion years. It has a diamond-like geometrical quality, is very similar in clarity and is said to be one of the few stones to rival true diamonds. Metaphysically, or in occult lore on stones, the Herkimer is associated with the activation of the third eye or Ajna chakra, which increases one's visionary capacity. In fact, the American Indians actually used Herkimers as "dream stones." It may well have been the peep stone used by Smith but it is difficult to ascertain at this stage, thanks to the Church's befuddling of the issue by having described the stones as being everything from crystal-clear to chocolate-colored.

How does all this pertain to a Ouija board? If we had to distinguish the difference between the average person who uses the Ouija board and the magician, it would be the faculty of Abrac. It all boils down to the average individual opening a doorway that allows them to wallow in the lower astral plane, which is often equated with Yesod or the Moon on the Qabalistic Tree of Life, while Abrac symbolizes a doorway opened in Tiphereth, the Sun, wherein higher entities, like angels, are allowed to descend.

Now, I'm not saying that with a lower elemental you cannot produce remarkable things; many of the authors cited possibly worked with astral entities, but it's hard to determine without accurate magickal records. While, hopefully, the reaching of the solar doorway and opening of this portal is the end goal, for most this is years away at best. First, we must learn about the lower astral. It is the easiest realm to open, but it is a realm that can often lead an untrained magician astray if they're not careful. However, all magicians *must* learn about and master this elemental domain.

The more "white-light" or religiously blinded might argue otherwise, cautioning you to avoid this "demonic realm of darkness" and seek only the Light. They believe you should avoid the lower Lunar realms of Hecate and seek only the Sun. However, magicians believe you must learn about the realm of the lower elementals. You must go through the darkness before you can see the Light. You must learn to face, vanquish and utilize all of one's own phantoms.

Returning to the subject of producing poetry, manuscripts and books through the Ouija board, Mrs. Hester Travers Smith, a psychic researcher, wrote about this phenomenon in her unique, honest and healthily skeptical little volume *Voices from the Void*, which appeared in 1919. She wrote how remarkable it was to witness an actual story being woven through a Ouija board, "the amazing rapidity with which the pattern of the plot develops; the traveller flies from letter to letter, seldom pausing for a word; the story reveals itself quite as quickly as if one were telling a well-known tale. It would be flattering to believe that this is a mere awakening of latent creative power in the sitters; I cannot credit the idea. These plots are certainly not in the consciousness of the mediums. At these sittings one is reminded of deep-sea fishing; one cannot predict whether a flatfish, an eel, or a whiting will be drawn up by the line. Some of these tales are modern, some are ancient; most of them are melodramatic, some very original. I am convinced that they come through an external influence, though they may be tinged by the medium's literary taste."[13] All in all, she agrees, as I do, that further study is needed in this area, "whether one admits the presence of an influence outside the medium or attributes this phenomenon to an abnormal quickening of the medium's creative power in a state of semi-hypnosis."[14]

Even if you don't believe in an external entity affecting the movement of the planchette and you acknowledge that it's only yourself functioning at a deeper level, isn't this worth developing? Especially considering that Aleister Crowley wrote that one's own personal Holy Guardian Angel may be little more than your Higher Self or own genius as yet manifested.

Hugh Lynn Cayce, the son of Edgar Cayce, believed that it is the individual who moves the triangle, explaining: "The information that generally comes through is just about what would be expected from the subconscious mind into which all kinds of thoughts have been pushed and suppressed. The product of such efforts can be a bewildering blend of nonsense, filth, and homespun philosophy. Fortunately, in most instances the result is weariness and impatience and the discovery is of little help and frequently exceedingly dull."[15] He continues, agreeing with Smith, that a small percentage of people who persist in using a Ouija board discover deeper levels "from which come poetic prose or poetry and frequently a great many religious admonitions."

Like many who have researched the board, he believes that certain individuals have the ability to tap into creative levels of their own subconscious through its use. I disagree as to whether their creative levels are being tapped into unconsciously or guided by some external being; it is believed that the deeper one goes into the astral waters, the finer the line of distinction becomes between what is "them" and us. Some magicians even claim that it is almost impossible to tell the difference whether you or an astral entity is controlling the planchette, and that in truth such a distinction is not necessary.

The scientific community tends to dismiss the premise that the planchette moves by some external means guided by angels, invisible beings or elementals, placing the origin of the planchette's movement solely within the individual's own subconscious mind, and feeling far more comfortable acknowledging psychic ability and ESP rather than invisible entities of God's Kingdoms. After all, God is not real to many individuals in our present-day society, but a metaphor. To state otherwise implies that one must accept all the invisible beings rumored to exist in his Kingdom. That would open an immense can of worms for modern society. It is far easier to simply claim that we should not confuse the issue with stories about invisible beings and that, in fact, it's just something that the individuals themselves are doing, end of subject. But invisible beings are real and can enter into an individual's unconscious, as any medium will attest. Whether the outcome is spirit communication, moving the triangle of a Ouija board or simply tapping into psychic energies, the end result is still the same. Something external to our constitution is moving through our psychic system. It is not always our subconscious acting out a wish fulfillment.

Actually, it is well known amongst ceremonial magicians that an individual can become one with any spirit by invoking the force of that deity into themselves. In this case the magician subjectively identifies himself with the force that has been called forth. The reasons for inducing this form of possession vary, but it usually occurs when a magician invokes something that he, or she, feels is lacking in their own constitution. The end result is that the magician strengthens his character.

Many books dealing with ceremonial magick approach the subject from this level, although few prepare the reader for any success as a vehicle and for what this really implies, forgetting the old axiom that if you don't fix the crack in the bottle first, the milk will spill out upon the floor. Everyone must prepare their psychic anatomy for the influx of new currents.

Contrary to what some would have you believe, you are not born with this ability. The method of subjective magick, or invoking forces to strengthen one's character, is not easily achieved with a Ouija board, and in fact is not recommended at all unless with the help and supervision of a well-trained magician. The dangers are very apparent as the possibility that personal obsession or possession is negatively reinforced rather than positively. The true story behind *The Exorcist* is a classic example of entities (or forces) that have possessed individuals after being unleashed through the Ouija board. While some might call these forces demonic or evil, they are neither. The proclivities of an individual's religious perceptions should not be blamed upon invisible entities that are merely trying to fulfill a person's unconscious wants, desires or even fears.

To be safe, one should always animate the board by evoking the entity into the triangle, or planchette, and then commanding it to remain there throughout the ritual. It should never be drawn through or into an individual. This cannot be stressed strongly enough. The key is the difference between the terms "invoke" and "evoke." Nothing is more confusing or contradictory than the use of these two terms. Aleister Crowley attempted to make the distinction between them easily understood when he wrote "To invoke is to call in, just as to evoke is to call forth."[16]

However, the magickal euphemism "As Above, So Below" implies that both evocation and invocation not only deal with personal spiritual attainment, but also with external methods of calling up real entities. The differences between the two methods are actually quite simple. When discussing the terms invoke and evoke in regard to personal attainment, one is referring to two distinct methods of Higher Magick. With invocation, universal forces are summoned from above to flood the consciousness. While using the term evocation, the magician identifies himself as the universe and dredges from the depths of his own subconscious certain dormant forces required to balance his imperfections. Both of these methods use the magician as the vehicle.

When we use these terms to discuss communication with actual invisible entities or angels, invocation implies that one is communicating with a disincarnated being through the use of a seer or psychic. In the most drastic cases it is through possession itself—the entity is invoked into, or through, an actual person in order to communicate. This could be very dangerous to the untrained and is not recommended. Evocation implies that the magician is summoning an entity into an external vehicle other than the magician, like a Ouija board or a magickal triangle. It is also arguable that the terms imply the direction from which an entity is summoned. If an invisible being is summoned from planes above our earth, then one is invoking him down from the universe. If the entity is bound upon this plane, or whose origin is below our plane, then we evoke him up from his depths. Invocation draws down while evocation draws up.

Regrettably, this attitude tends to lump invisible beings into either an angel or a demon category. The terms are confusing depending upon whom you're reading; even Crowley, throughout his many books, tends to befuddle the terms, as do most magicians. When reflecting upon these two terms in relationship to a Ouija board one should always evoke or call forth an entity. Crowley wrote, "You invoke a God into a Circle. You evoke a Spirit into the Triangle."[17] With this in mind, the nature of the Ouija is obvious. The planchette, or pointer, of a Ouija board, is shaped like a triangle. This indicates the true nature of the board and its use as a tool to evoke or manifest forces.

In some ways it is regrettable that the talking board was made into a popular game. Its full potential has never been taken seriously. With so many different studies by researchers, psychologists and parapsychologists who believe the board to be little more than the ramblings of an unconscious mind, trying to restore, or elevate, a Ouija board to its rightful status as a spiritual tool capable of bridging the worlds is often difficult. Though many authorities associate the talking board with disincarnated entities and have done so for a long time, they often deny it and evade making the assumption publicly.

Few individuals have attempted honest research in regard to the Ouija board. Most writers approach the subject from the tainted viewpoint of a witness or researcher on the subject, rather than attempting a more hands-on attitude by actually using the board themselves to determine its validity. One person who actually used the board for the basis of her research was Mrs. Hester Travers Smith, whom I briefly mentioned earlier. She published many of her experiments in *Voices from the Void*, wherein she writes more as a sitter who experiences the board first-hand rather than an observer who tends to view what is being seen with skepticism. Like most mediums of her period, she did not like the mass-produced Ouija boards, calling them the "apparatus for which can be purchased in any children's toy-shop in the 'games' department."[18] Her argument was that the "planchette is the clumsiest, most primitive, and least satisfactory 'autoscope' possible, and I should recommend anyone who desires to experiment in this field of research to avoid this particular method."[19]

It is believed the real reason why many mediums of her day hated to use the store-bought Ouija board is that it further "cheapened" their art, which was already under suspicion through nothing less than pure ignorance. Mediums also tried to downplay the Ouija board's ability, hoping to steer the public away from their bread-and-butter trade. If everyone could do it, who would pay exorbitant prices to a medium? Regardless, like many mediums, Smith preferred the standard version of the talking board that was used around the turn of the century, describing it in depth in her book. "The best Ouija-board, the one I invariably use myself, is a card table covered with green baize, on which the letters of the alphabet, the numbers 0 to

9, and the words 'yes' and 'no' are laid, cut out separately on small pieces of cardboard; over this is placed a sheet of plate glass, the same size as the table. The traveller consists of a small triangular piece of wood, about half an inch thick, shod with three small pieces of carpet felt and having on top a piece of soft rubber material on which the fingers rest."[20]

Her book is filled with many opinions that are held sacred by researchers regarding the Ouija board. For instance, when she questions herself as to whether or not she was moving the board unconsciously, she writes with honesty, "The crux in deciding whether or not an external influence is at work consists in determining how far the subliminal self plays a part in these experiments. No one present is in a more difficult position to judge of this that the automatist himself. When at the board I am not conscious that my condition is other than normal, but if I were asked whether or not I used my hand to push the traveller to certain letters I should be quite unable to reply. If I do this, it is an entirely subconscious action on my part. What I can state confidently is, that after a short time messages come through my brain before they are written down, and I am again unable to say whether they are suggestions from an external entity or not. I am inclined to believe they are. For sometimes sentences come through which are quite contrary to what I should expect, and again, when I am most desirous that the traveller should move for me, it stands stock-still."[21]

In her own summary of the Ouija, she acknowledges that what "makes any definite pronouncement on this subject almost impossible is that, no matter what theory one holds, it is difficult to adhere to it rigidly, for the simple reason that, although the results of nine sittings might be accounted for by our subliminal self or telepathy, at the tenth sitting something may occur which upsets and puzzles us and leads us to believe that, after all, something supernormal has got possession of us."[22] Anyone who has worked the board over a lengthy period of time will agree with her conclusions. However, one doesn't need ten sittings to achieve communication with a disincarnated entity. Under proper control through ceremonial magick, results are almost immediate and all the time.

Still, even knowing that a Ouija board can be used properly, it is doubtful that Ed or Lorraine Warren would ever recommend its use. It's obvious that they're terrified of it, and they are not alone; their views are shared by many, and in some ways we should not criticize them or hold them accountable for their religious fears. Ed Warren states, "The Ouija board opens the doors to the supernatural, to supernatural attack ... (When) you use the Ouija board, you're communicating with an invisible, intangible realm, and negative spirits can enter through the board."[23] Most researchers agree with his comments, but magicians are not so quick at board burning. There is, in fact, a correct way of using the Ouija board. Mrs. Hester Travers Smith gives sound advice: "be patient, be prudent, never let an unbalanced or hysterical person be present at your sittings; be satisfied with small results and look for nothing sensational, work regularly and do not let dull sittings discourage you. With caution and wisdom much may be achieved."[24] Crowley points out, "There is, however, a good way of using this instrument to get what you want ... so that undesirable aliens cannot interfere with it."[25]

How the board works is one of the great debates of our time. Most writings on the subject tend to acknowledge the board as a means of tapping only into the subconscious, and none until now has revealed what some people have suspected all along: the spirit world exists, as well as all its hosts, both good and evil. You might be prompted to run out and purchase a Ouija board to discover this Truth for yourself. If you do, be sure to read carefully the blurb on the back of the box: "Ouija ... is only a game ... isn't it?"

CHAPTER FOUR

"Apollonius must certainly have made the closest links between his Ruach and his Supernal Triad, and this would have gone seeking a new incarnation elsewhere. All the available Ruach left floating around in the Akasha must have been comparatively worthless odds and ends, true Qliphoth or 'Shells of the Dead'—just those parts of him, in a word, which Apollonius would have deliberately discarded at his death."

—ALEISTER CROWLEY

People can communicate with an astounding diversity of beings through a Ouija board. The average person usually wants to talk with a deceased relative or a ghost whom they believe is haunting their house. We need to explore this theory by asking ourselves if it is really plausible.

Spiritualists have profited by claiming that they can communicate with the spirits of the deceased. Aleister Crowley paints a nice picture when referring to one such "modern Spiritist in the dingy squalor of her foul back street in her suburban slum, the room musty, smelling of stale food, the hideous prints, the cheap and rickety furniture, calling up any one required from Jesus Christ to Queen Victoria."[1] The Great Beast was not kind, especially when he sums up his views on the subject of Spiritism with just one word: "Faugh!" Crowley did not appreciate this topic or its methods in the least. This is a shame, for he condemned a valuable tool simply because of the incompetence of its users. Then again, he grew up in a period when spiritists were a dime a dozen, vampirizing the public similar to the phone psychics of today.

The belief in ghosts is widespread throughout our world. Many people honestly believe they have lived in a haunted house and have seen or heard things that have gone bump in the night. They may convince themselves that the ghost might be a deceased relative who, having unfinished business, is simply returning to complete a task. This belief helps appease our sanity by allowing us to think that it's perhaps our kith and kin whose troubled spirit roams the house. Even the mere idea that the invisible entity was once an actual human reassures us that if we can communicate with it, as we could when it was alive, we can persuade it to stop haunting.

People who believe in ghosts have little understanding of the invisible kingdoms or their own spiritual anatomy: when we die, our divine spirit goes on, reincarnates and continues the life cycle. This is not to say that occasionally, after death, a spirit cannot descend briefly into our world to complete a specific task before moving on. However, what is spiritually illogical is the concept that through one insensitive act of peak emotion or violence by some madman, a beautiful spirit can be bound to the earth for all eternity, while the perpetrator of the crime goes free to reincarnate at will. If there were a God, why would he penalize the innocent victim of a heinous crime instead of trying to rescue their tormented spirit? Even if it was the person's own insensitive act which caused their own demise, why would a God ignore them—and even if you don't believe in reincarnation, why would a God, any God, abandon one of his flock when he has legions of angels whose task it is to watch over our Earth in order to protect us and guide us? That mere mortals who are good religious people are expected by their faith to help others in distress in society, while God's angels are allowed to stand by and do nothing to save a spirit if it becomes lost or confused, doesn't make any sense. The average ghost must be something other than a divine human spirit.

Regardless of logic, attempting to communicate with the deceased through a Ouija board is common. Aleister Crowley has written that it is not easy to summon the spirit of the deceased for numerous reasons, but he acknowledges "what can be done is to pick up the astral remains of the dead man from the Akasha and to build them up into a concrete mind. This operation, again, is not particularly profitable."[2] He is correct; it is certainly not easy to communicate with the deceased, especially if its spirit has already reincarnated. (Of course, there are those who might disagree with his assertion that communicating with an astral remnant is "not profitable.") The astral remnant that Crowley mentions is what we shall discuss in this chapter.

First of all, what most people call a ghost is what magicians like Crowley refer to as the "Shells of the Dead."[3] The Shell itself is just what the name implies: hollow and without conscious direction. The great debate amongst magicians, philosophers and religious scholars is what exactly remains and what a spirit keeps when it incarnates. I do not agree with the concept that a Shell is merely "worthless odds and ends" or those parts of an individual that the Spirit has decided to discard upon the death of its mortal vehicle. I agree more with Eastern philosophy which states that a Shell is the sum total of an individual's incarnation. Upon death, an individual does not pick and choose which parts they'd like to keep and throw away the rest like old clothes. This is an old aeonic or Christian concept based upon the idea that only the good can enter into the kingdom of Heaven.

A spirit incarnates for the whole experience and it takes out the sum total of such, whether it is bathed in good or evil. The confusion for most lies in that everything below what is called the Abyss on the Qabalistic Tree of Life is a form of energy bathed in duality. The Ruach or central ego of every individual is not exempt from this quality. Some religious-minded individuals would like to simply divide everything into two categories of black or white, believing that all the good goes on while the evil remains, but this portrays a lack of understanding of what duality implies.

All experience gained below the Abyss, especially from the point of view of Malkuth or our Earth, is nothing more than obtaining Knowledge—which is merely a form of energy and as such it can never dissipate. Qabalists allegorically will tell you that Knowledge is a Serpent originating from Malkuth that is unable to venture beyond the Abyss into a new incarnation. When a spirit incarnates, or moves into the Abyss, the energy or experience, being a spawn of duality, splits and mutates. That which moves above the Abyss becomes a form of Understanding. In other words, the sum total of the experience for which the spirit had incarnated is preserved and taken away onto this next plane. The spirit does not "forget" or discard some things while remembering others. It simply "understands" all of its incarnation and accepts all that is and has been as part of the whole experience. There is no pain of division or importance placed on one thing over another.

What stays below the Abyss does such without a spirit. This is why Knowledge is called a Shell, and why Qabalists say it wears a false Crown. It has no spiritual guidance but, like that which is taken above the Abyss, Knowledge contains the sum total of an individual's incarnation. It is often difficult to grasp what is occurring because there can never be a coherence below the Abyss which implies transcending the duality. Focus on what you think something becomes and automatically the mind becomes befuddled by thinking of its opposite. Reasoning breaks it into pieces, and you'll find yourself walking out the back door in search of answers, only to knock on the front door so that you can be let in to be shown the back door again. Magicians call this being lost in the Abyss.

What exactly is a Shell that is left in a spirit's wake? This is the question that concerns us. It is said that everything that has ever been thought or done, every single event no matter how trivial, is a form of energy that is eternally recorded in time within a given Shell. This Shell resides in the astral waters around our Earth. The Shell is merely a concept that encases a certain type of energy (Knowledge). To understand the concept of the Shell better, consider it like a record being played on a phonograph. The person who has done the recording has gone on to do other things, as in the case of a spirit incarnating, but do they forget everything about the experience of the recording session? Of course not, yet his record, or Shell, can be played over and over again. Like a phonograph record, this realm is two-sided, containing the good and evil of all things.

Although some refer to the records in height and depth rather than two sides, both analogies are correct. The astral may even be likened to an immense computer whose memory is just waiting to be opened with the push of a button. Some religious fraternities believe these records can only be read or revealed at special times, and only to specially trained or enlightened individuals who have learned astral travel. This is not true. Crowley felt, like many Old Aeonic Qabalists, that the Shells of individuals are merely the negative discharges remaining after the individual has reincarnated. He considered such to be "worthless odds and ends,"[4] and wondered why anyone such as a Spiritist would even bother to tap into them, questioning, "So what use would they be?"[5] However, in his hatred toward Spiritists he forgets the wealth of information and guidance that can be obtained by the reading the astral records, *especially one's own*. These records are the Cosmic Chronicles of human destiny. A trained magician can unravel his own records like a ribbon into the past, present and even into the future. Previously we mentioned such qualities of time are attributed to the god Apollo; we must never forget this God or the invisible oracles that are known as the Dactyls. They shall play an important role in our investigation of the realms between.

Magicians should not be contemptuous about the methods that mediums use to tap into these records. It's the inane questions their clientele ask that degrade the subject to its lowest common denominator. As an example, when meeting a great man who is still alive, one is prone to ask pertinent questions so that one's moment might be richly rewarded. After all, one doesn't get the opportunity every day; time should be precious and not wasted on trivial pursuits. Yet why do we forget this when communicating with his Shell through a Ouija board after such a person has died? This is an important lesson that everyone should learn when communicating with Shells.

When I was first learning this art, my own teacher informed me that the single most important thing in attempting any form of communication is to learn what to say and how to carefully word it. How many magicians do elaborate rituals seeking money, only to find a penny? The wording of magickal affirmations is paramount, and the questions one asks through a Ouija board are equally important. Most tragedies can be traced back to this single most repeated error when using the board.

At this point you might be asking yourself, "If they're not ghosts, then why do Shells haunt houses?" The answer to this is actually quite simple and common magickal sense. Our plane is considered positive by its mundane nature and Shells are referred to as being a negative discharge, which Crowley acknowledged. Our Divine Spirit is neutrally charged. Each type, within itself, contains both positive and negative currents in order to exist, although one current is usually stronger than the other. Note that the term "negative" does not necessarily imply the negation of all positive qualities; magickally referring to a negative quality is simply referring to an opposite or mirror image.

A negative quality is not necessarily evil, unless its positive was evil. As an example, when you look into a mirror you see a reflection of yourself. This is a negative quality, or Shell, in contrast to the actual positive person standing in front of the mirror. The negative image has no consciousness. Only you have consciousness because you have a spirit. If you're a kind person, then the reflection in the mirror does not reverse into becoming some evil, hideous and grotesque monster; it is merely a reflection or Shell of the reality.

Returning to the question why Shells haunt houses, we previously discussed that a Shell is little more than negative records that have been impressed upon the astral plane by an individual throughout his or her life. Most individuals, when nearing death, accept their fate and shed their earthly vehicle without trauma. However, there are times when severe emotional tragedies such as those resulting in murder or suicide, or simply deep regrets at the point of death, cause a last-minute "recorded message" to be impressed on the astral waters, reflecting that the person really doesn't want to die or leave others behind. If it is an extremely strong negative charge then the Shell could be attracted to its opposite or the most positive charged place on the mind of the Spirit at the point of its death. In cases of a violent death these Shells could be drawn to the last place the body and spirit coexisted together. This is the truth behind ghosts: they are simply Shells manifesting.

Another myth often fostered through ignorance is that you can communicate directly with the Shell, either through a psychic or through a specially trained individual. You cannot talk with a Shell. The Shell itself is simply a movie or image being played over and over again. Although certain people can view these records, such readings are often tainted by the vehicle or medium that is doing the viewing; the medium may "see" what is easiest for them to view, rather than what the client really requests. These readings may or may not have any bearing on anything—one individual used the analogy that it's like placing a needle in the middle of a phonograph record in order to see what plays.

If a Shell is just a record of events, then with whom do people communicate when using a Ouija board? The Shell of a deceased person, or their energy discarded at death, is what other invisible beings animate and use as a magical link to cross over into our world. These beings are far older than our human race. They've been around since time began, born in the bowels of every hill, deep in our Earth, neither having a mother or a father nor being male or female themselves. They are all around us and certain areas, like sacred spots and even some homes, act as a thinly veiled doorway whereby they can traverse between the planes. These entities are called elementals. The ancient Greeks called them Dactyls. In Arabic they are known as the genii that, according to legend, ruled the Earth before the creation of Adam. Others, like witches, call them familiars. They have been known by numerous names throughout history and whether they are considered good or evil depends upon the culture that is telling the story.

Although they are called by different names, the stories are usually similar. They tell of an ancient race of invisible beings that can be summoned to help us, guide us and do our bidding. The ancient fables and stories equally warn us against the misuse of such power that is placed in our *hands*. They tell graphic tales of these entities turning on those who have summoned them, tricking them and causing great harm to the unsuspecting fool who has ventured into their grasp. These entities are truly shape-shifters. They are neither good nor evil. It is relatively safe and fairly easy to allow them to animate a Shell. This literally means that they *become* that which you're seeking. Crowley further elaborated by calling them "... tricksters, of the lowest elemental orders" who "come and vitalize odds and ends of the Ruach of people recently deceased, and perform astonishing impersonations."[6]

However, we shall also discuss throughout this book the dangers in letting one of these invisible beings run free on our plane through a Ouija board, and how they can become the poltergeists which can haunt our homes and manifest our worst nightmares. Control is mandatory, and every culture that has mentioned these beings is in agreement with this simple fact.

There are great advantages in understanding all this. We can directly communicate with the elemental who has become the sum total of the Shell's experience. By doing this we can learn anything we desire to know. Also, by communicating through an elemental, we don't have to view indiscriminate records until we find what we need. We let the elemental do this. If we were to consider the astral records or Shells as the main files in a computer, the elemental is simply our "search" mechanism. Because of this nature some magicians feel more comfortable referring to the elemental as a go-between. What a ghost-buster or medium does when they seemingly convince a "ghost" to stop haunting is also simple, though most do not realize that they achieve this task through an elemental that goes into the astral records, finds the repeated "skip" and simply removes it, similar to a skip on a phonograph record. In other words, the elemental can shift the negative energy into a more even flow, rather than having it "bunched up" at a person's death in a strong last-minute recorded message. Without this strong charge, the Shell can no longer manifest in a repeated cycle.

When the house is no longer haunted, the "ghost" is freed and the medium may believe that it was he or she who has convinced the poor deceased individual to let go. If they only knew the whole truth, or were trained properly, they could achieve far more using magickal techniques. Most psychics and mediums do not understand the darker shades of the invisible kingdoms, often blindly achieving their goals protected by their own ignorance.

There *are* dangers: when animating Shells a serious error often occurs. Never forget the Shell itself is not real in the sense of being a deceased person—it is only animated and used as a doorway by an elemental. Even if it tells you otherwise, don't believe it. The elemental can only tell you what you want to know and, if you start unconsciously believing the Shell is a deceased person, then the elemental will agree and fulfill your wish by claiming to be such. This often occurs through a Ouija board where an individual begins placing the Shell on a pedestal as if it were a higher spiritual being than themselves.

This can foster serious problems. You might tend to think that such a person will play by earthly rules, similar to when he or she was alive. This is totally wrong and can be outright dangerous: the elemental's actions, if left unchecked, can be disastrous because it will play by the rules of its plane, not yours! It can shape-shift into your worst fears and nightmares. In fact, most elementals feed off fear or other heightened emotions; I cannot stress this strongly enough. If you drop your guard and unleash an elemental from the tethers that bind it within the triangle, although it is basically passive by nature, by that exact same nature it will automatically try to take charge of its surroundings and you could be swamped with poltergeist activity. However, an elemental can only give you exactly, to the letter, what *you* want, and because of this desperately tries to fulfill what it strongly believes to be your desires, even if you're unconsciously aware of such. Magician, know thyself!

CHAPTER FIVE

"March 8th, the strange noyse in my chamber of knockings; and the voyce, ten tymes repeted, somewhat like the shrich of an owle, but more longly drawn, and more softly, as it were in my chamber."

—JOHN DEE

The greatest danger when using a Ouija board is the assumption that one will automatically investigate spiritual realms when laying one's hands upon the planchette. To acquire a mastery of the faculty of Abrac which allows us to connect with the Sun is far more difficult than it may seem. Once free of our mundane world, we enter into a vast elemental realm where virtually anything is created merely by thinking, both consciously and unconsciously. Contrary to what some might like you to believe, it is neither a mythic realm nor is it the fabrication of dreams. It is merely a realm beyond our normal senses, whose Laws of creation are achieved in a manner different than things in the mundane. More shocking is the realization that life, albeit different than our own, exists in this realm independent of us. All around us are numerous classifications of invisible beings that do not need our permission to be there. They float in and out of our rooms, walk our stairs and traverse the hidden byways of our homes. Like insects crawling through tiny passages, these entities exist even though we cannot see them. Some of them are good while others are dangerous, if not outright evil. Numerous types of entities populate the realms between, living an existence which allows them to drift between their world and ours at their convenience or whenever beckoned.

To not fall sway to interpreting other people's wants in regard to God's kingdom, we shall deal first with the origins of entities known as the lower elementals, exploring their realm and its structure. It is the closest realm to ours and easiest to enter. Also, it must be mastered before attempting to go deeper. Some of the most accepted road maps or theories about this realm come from the teachings found in both Hinduism and Buddhism. These beliefs are that elemental life streams forth, not necessarily *from* but *through* our Sun as subtle currents or waves known as Tattwas. These invisible tides contain not only the archetypal life forms known as lower elementals, which are normally attracted to a Ouija board like moths to a light bulb, but also a plethora of other beings who surf these waves as if it were their highway, from angels to the demons of our myths and fears.

The concept that the Sun is a doorway is neither new nor restricted to Eastern thought. Western magicians have known for centuries that this solar orb is paramount in regard to communion with other spiritual beings. We've already noted that Masons call this the faculty of Abrac, or the knowledge of the power and use of the mystical solar god Abraxas. In fact, the Sun is known as Tiphereth on the ancient Hebrew Qabalistic Tree of Life. It is also considered to be the sphere in which one accomplishes the knowledge of and conversation with their personal Holy Guardian Angel. Yet on another, more simplistic, level, within this Solar alchemical furnace a process begins which allows the fibers of life on our planet, including humans, to be brought to birth. We call the manifested quality of this invisible life force sunlight. Without this force all life as we know it dies. However, with every aspect of manifestation there is also a subtle invisible quality that bathes our Earth. These invisible solar tides or Tattwas are known as Vayu, Tejas,

Apas and Prithivi. They are attributed to the four elemental qualities of Air, Fire, Water and Earth.

As to our divine spirit's origin beyond the Sun, this is a question religions must answer. Philosophers have long believed that, like the tides, our spirit enters through the Sun in quest of an incarnation and that this sphere is also the source of "light" that individuals see during a near-death experience. The Sun acts as a gateway into our mundane universe, and one by which our spirit is allowed to exit upon death. In all cases, incarnation is accomplished by traversing the elemental highway also known as the astral plane. Elementals in these astral waters will incarnate and manifest their archetypal structures in relationship to the magician's needs and spiritual upbringing. After all, this lower elemental or Lunar world is a pliable dreamscape and will take the shape of whatever we impress upon it, especially unconsciously. Thelemically, "every man and every woman is a star" (*Liber AL vel Legis* I:3) and the light of our inner Sun, when cast downward into the Lunar waters, creates images or shadows. We must learn to recognize our own unconscious creations and not fall sway to them as if they are Divine Guidance. This is a valuable lesson that everyone must learn when attempting to use a Ouija board.

Once into the astral realm, if one sees loathsome, monstrous and hideous shapes it is often easy to banish them into the farthest reaches so that they do you no harm on your journey. However, it is far harder to recognize that danger comes in all shapes. Again, magicians, know thyselves. The greatest danger is not clothed in the foul and detestable, but found in the images of an unconscious wish fulfillment from an often-failed reality, which tempts you into a false sense of importance. What both the unsightly and the beautiful have in common is that they are merely shadows cast by one's own star. The goal is not to wallow in either of these shadows, but rather to utilize that which creates them, the Sunlight or solar currents, in order to reach our Holy Guardian Angel.

The best Western system on this subject of solar currents, which in many ways mimics Eastern thought, is the Enochian system of magick. It is a complicated system and we can give only an overview of certain aspects. In the Enochian system, as in Buddhism and Hinduism, the Sun plays an integral or central role in the manifestation of the fibers that comprise the invisible world around our Earth. In the first chapter I mentioned the Elizabethan magician, John Dee, who looked into the invisible realms through the use of a crystal ball. Here the entities or angels appeared and communicated their messages by pointing to one letter at a time on a huge board of letters. The same principle holds true for the Ouija board but, instead of going within the invisible realms, we bring the entities out into our world to communicate in the same fashion, allowing them to move the triangle from one letter to another in order to spell out messages.

It is believed that John Dee became interested in magic while studying at Cambridge as a young man around 1542, but it wasn't until he settled into his family's estate at Mortlake years later that the system of angelic magic began to appear. Dee had an overzealous religious thirst for knowledge, and immersed himself in religious thought, prayers and study, often rejecting organized churches as a middleman between humanity and God. In many ways he was a true Gnostic in his belief that every individual has the ability to personally obtain the Gnosis if he or she is spiritually ready to perceive the Truth. His ambitions were to establish contact with the same angels who had descended throughout history to God's chosen, like the Biblical prophet Enoch who was the first human to talk with the angels after the fall of Adam and Eve. It is from the name Enoch that the title Enochian magick is later derived, because John Dee, like Enoch, communicated with the four great archangels Michael, Uriel, Raphael, and Gabriel, as well as a host of other entities. During his own lifetime Dee simply referred to his system as Angelic.

The term "archangel" is often used without awareness of its celestial meaning or implication. According to numerous religious sources, Heaven is comprised of many Celestial Halls, each of a higher spiritual stage than the previous. The term archangel is applied generically to all spiritual beings residing in the Kingdom or Hall directly above the class of beings known as the angels, who are directly above mankind. There are varying types of archangels with different tasks and abilities. The four archangels mentioned above are of the class referred to as the *Egoroi* or *Grigori*, which simply means the Watchers. According to biblical text such as The Book of Jubilees, the Watchers were sent down to Earth to guide humanity and instruct the children of men who were spiritually ready to perceive their divine messages or Gnosis, which, of course, came directly from God.

It was these archangels of Light that John Dee sought. He wrote that he had "often read in thy (God's) books and records, how Enoch enjoyed thy favour and conversation; with Moses thou was familiar; And also that to Abraham, Isaack and Jacob, Joshua, Gideon, Esdras, Daniel, Tobias and sundry others thy good angels were sent by thy disposition, to Instruct them, informe them, helpe them, yea in worldly and domestick affaires, yea and sometymes to satisfie their desires, doubtes, and questions of thy Secrete: And Furdermore considering, the Shewstone, which the High Prieste did use, by thy owne ordering ... that this wisdome could not be come by at man's hand or by humaine power, but only from thee"[1], or rather, from God.

It is presumed that Dee's earliest attempt to converse with the angels occurred in March of 1581 when he began being troubled by strange dreams as well as knockings and rappings throughout his house at Mortlake. In his *Private Diaries* he records that he heard on "March 8th, the strange noyse in my chamber of knockings; and the voyce, ten tymes repeted, somewhat like the shrich of an owle, but more longly drawn, and more softly, as it were in my chamber."[2] He further records on August 3rd that the strange knockings and rappings in his chamber returned and plagued him all night, and on the following night too. In our day and age one might suspect a poltergeist or elemental had been unleashed by a person's tampering with the occult, but John Dee interpreted these occurrences as an angel trying to communicate some divine message. He viewed the visitations with awe and was humbly willing to do anything God commanded if only he could figure out what it was. Such religious sincerity is found throughout his diaries. It has been suggested that the key to Enochian magic is found in the manner by which this man poured out his soul, a lesson one should heed well before attempting such magick, even with the Ouija board.

In his early attempts to communicate with the entity behind the knockings and rappings, a Shewstone or crystal was used for spirit vision. It became an intricate part of his experiments. Many believe that Dee himself lacked the ability of clairvoyant sight, often employing Seers or Mediums to make contact with the spiritual beings that he was summoning through his prayers and spiritual evocations. This is not completely true. He does record, for instance, that on May 25th, 1581, "I had sight in crystall offered me, and I saw,"[3] which implies that he had some ability at skrying. Other times he records visions in which he heard thunder, roaring and trumpet sounds.

We can only speculate as to why he sought out the aid of others. Most of these Seers failed, even his first, Barnabas Saul, whose visions were said to be extremely inferior. There is also some indication that the strange sounds and noises around Mortlake were taking their toll on Saul's sanity. In one diary entry on October 9th, 1581, Dee records that he found Barnabas Saul lying in the hall "strangely troubled by a spirituall creature abowt mydnight." [4] Dee's family home must have been a fun place late at night! Much to the regret of John Dee, the following year Barnabas Saul recanted everything by claiming that he made up all his visions. It is presumed by most historians that his confession was based on fear of being persecuted as a sorcerer; being charged with heresy or witchcraft had a way of making a man recant his personal beliefs. John Dee's diaries record that on March 1st, 1582, Barnabas Saul appeared at Mortlake and "confessed that he neyther hard or saw any spirituall creature any more."[5]

After this John Dee went through a succession of such failures with Seers, including his own son. He felt that most of the angelic visions were obviously tainted by the Seers' inability to act as a channel and that they were simply unconsciously manipulating everything they saw—the visions did not reflect higher spiritual, or angelic, qualities that Dee had so hoped to receive from God. The same problem can occur when using a Ouija board: the two people whose hands are placed upon the triangle may have to be replaced often until suitable mediums can be found who can channel a vision and not unconsciously interfere with what is being received. In Dee's case a suitable medium appeared on March 9th in 1582. He was Mr. Edward Talbot, who shortly thereafter changed his name, for reasons unknown, to Edward Kelly.

John Dee was different from most Elizabethan magicians of his period. He avoided doing magic based on singular achievements. With each new day he built upon the previous experiment by asking the angels themselves what they required next, and recorded everything in his diaries in minutest detail. He listened to these visions, prayed and constantly asked for guidance, claiming that the "key of Prayer openeth all things."[6] In many ways he was a very religious and pious man—a lesson to learn in respect to one's own magick. A fleeting Ouija ritual done over a single night achieves little but, if continued properly over a lengthy period of time, one has the ability to open up the gates to the invisible world, especially if constantly asking the entities what is required next. In the early stages of any spiritual working you should determine how to fine-tune the ritual, throwing out the gross and elaborating upon that which works best.

There is no better way to determine this than by asking

the angels you've summoned, as John Dee did centuries earlier. Listen to the angels carefully and remember that no two ritualists will ever have the same requirements due to each person's differing spiritual growth and needs. It is important, however, to realize the difference between elementals and angels; they are not the same. One is a pliable arena of your unconscious desires while the other is an independent entity with its own agenda. You must work through one in order to lay a suitable foundation for the other to descend.

The paraphernalia that the angels required Dee to make are truly remarkable. In these early communications, John Dee was instructed in the proper construction of a specific table, along with seven talismans of tin known as "The Ensigns of Creation" to be used in conjunction with it. Later, a new Holy Twelvefold Table was constructed with the talismans painted directly upon it in blue lines with bright red letters. Of the actual coloring of the symbols on the table itself, very little is known. We do know that the letters around the edges of the table that comprised the fourteen names of certain angelic Kings and Princes, as well as the large letter B at each corner, were to be painted in yellow. A complete diagram of the Holy Twelvefold Table has appeared in many sources but the vast majority are incorrect renderings. Most, including Aleister Crowley's, use Meric Causabon as their source, but when comparing his diagram to Dee's original drawing found in the appendix to his *Liber Mysteriorum Quinta,* it is obvious that Causabon has many letters around the table's edge in the wrong place. Wading through Enochian magick is not as simple as picking up one book on the subject, as folly is often compounded upon previously printed folly.

John Dee was also given specific instructions on how to make an elaborately engraved wax talisman known as *Sigillum Dei Aemeth*, or Talisman of Truth. It was placed in the center of the Holy Table, then a huge red silken cloth was placed over the entire table, hanging down over the sides with tassels at each corner. A special Shewstone was acquired of quartz crystal, which Dee had set into a frame of solid gold and mounted upon a Calvary Cross. This, in turn, was placed upon the cloth covering the engraved wax talisman. There were other items, like the four smaller versions of Sigillum Dei Aemeth that were to be placed under the table's legs. There is mention that two more square yards of red silk was used here, but it is unclear whether the cloth goes on the floor itself, or was placed between the four smaller talismans and the table legs. The angels also gave instructions on how to make a specific breastplate of parchment and a magical ring, to name only a few of the many items.

John Dee was obsessed, sometimes doing rituals two or three times in a single day. Each time the angels revealed further mysteries as to what was required of him; each time the magician fulfilled the new obligations and asked what was next. Finally an entire system of angelic magick had been unveiled. Individuals who attempt Ouija workings should take heed of Dee's religious dedication.

Among the more perplexing items obtained fairly early were numerous tablets filled with squares, some with letters in the middle, while others were blank. However, most were 49 x 49 squares in measurement. These lettered boards, similar in some ways to a Ouija, would play a critical role in Enochian magick. For instance, when doing a particular working, Edward Kelly would kneel down before the Holy Table and the Shewstone. There were no special evocations or magical rituals to call forth the spirits outside of simple prayers. In some ways Ouija magick begins the same way by a person simply asking, "Is someone there?" After a while Kelly would report that an angel had appeared to him in the crystal along with a vision, which usually included one of the many tablets previously obtained. Once the tablet was determined, Dee would find it and place it upon the Holy Table. At this point Kelly would report that the angel was pointing to one of the squares on the tablet with his sacred wand, usually saying, as an example, that the square was in the third row over, fourth down. Dee in turn would locate the letter on the Tablet, which he had before him, and write it down.

This might seem like a laborious task, but John Dee realized the importance of doing it this way, stating "that unlesse of this strange language I should have these words delivered unto us Letter by Letter, we might erre both in Orthography, and also for want of the true pronunciation of the words, and distinctions of the points, we might more misse the effect expect."[7] Orthography, the study of correct spelling according to accepted usage of words, is something in which Dee was very learned for his period.

Another unique thing obtained by Dee and Kelly was an angelic alphabet that has come to be known as Enochian. It is very strange and all the letters on The Holy Table as well as the talisman and sacred tablets were to be written in this angelic tongue. In addition to this and the paraphernalia that the angels informed John Dee he must obtain or make, they also taught him the structure of their universe, known as the 30 Aethyrs or realms, often equated as celestial kingdoms. Each realm is ruled by a specific Governor and a host of other beings that could be summoned by one or more of 19 Keys or Calls. These evocations are probably the most powerful in the world. Israel Regardie has stated that the "genuineness of these Keys, altogether apart from any critical observation, is guaranteed by the fact that anyone with the smallest capacity for Magick finds that they work."[8] Originally these angelic Keys were written backwards, being far too dangerous to disclose in a straightforward manner. Afterward they had to be reversed to make sense out of what was written.

Enochian is an extremely complicated system. It plays an important role in this book on Ouija magick, and enables us to utilize the board to greater depths. I was once asked by a student, "Why are we bothering with the Enochian system with a Ouija Board?" I reminded him that although John Dee obtained much knowledge through his efforts, his system remained relatively unknown until present times. The reasons for this are intricate, but most scholars believe that somehow Dee's normal practices laid a foundation whereby this particular system of angelic magick, destined for the present Age of Aquarius, was wrested from the hands of the angels hundreds of years before its time. This, of course, occurred while the Age of Pisces was still bathing our world: the learned John Dee reached a pinnacle of Piscean magick through his studies and religious practices, and some believe it was inevitable that he saw into the future of magick. Whether or not he understood its full potential will always be debated.

The view that Enochian magick is an Aquarian system is confirmed by Aleister Crowley, who gave the modern world its first public glimpse of the system when he published aspects of it in *A Brief Abstract of The Symbolic Representation of The Universe Derived by Doctor John Dee through the Skrying of Sir Edward Kelly* in one of his laborious volumes of *The Equinox* in 1912. He had learned of Enochian magick while still an initiate in the fraternity The Hermetic Order of the Golden Dawn. In 1909, while Crowley was in Algeria, he attempted his own investigations of the Aethyrs, or subtle non-terrestrial abodes, which Dee had previously unfolded. While skrying in the 6th Aethyr, Crowley had an angelic vision whereby he was told that in "the Book of Enoch was first given the wisdom of the New Aeon. And it was hidden for three hundred years, because it was wrested untimely from the Tree of Life by the hand of a desperate magician."[9] It is believed that this is a reference to none other than Edward Kelly, John Dee's partner. It was Kelly who acted as the Seer while Dee wrote down everything he saw, and in fact the Great Beast claimed that one of his previous incarnations was none other than Kelly.

Because the system is intensely complicated, weighty and bathed in old English jargon, many students are often reluctant to study it, failing to realize that the majority of what we term John Dee's Enochian system is in fact Piscean or old aeonic magick. Very little of his manuscripts are required to study in order to make the system work effectively—the system is not important in the immensity of all its old aeonic literature, but in the simplicity of its usage in the new aeon. The same holds true when using the Ouija board.

CHAPTER SIX

"four very fair castles, standing in the four parts of the world: out of which he heard the sound of a Trumpeter."

—John Dee

We have been given a great gift with the Laws of Abrac which allow us to make a connection with the solar door within ourselves and externally. Crowley's followers, called Thelemites, are especially aware of the nature of the astral tides that stretch 93 million miles between our Earth and the Sun. John Dee, for all his accomplishments, was unaware of the system's full import. Of all his visions, one that he obtained through skrying lays the very foundation of our modern understanding of the elemental kingdom: the angels unfolded the mystery behind the solar door through which all God's hosts descend into our world, including lower elementals. This fourfold doorway is known as the Watchtowers, and their structure must be studied in depth because of their relationship with a Ouija board.

This may perplex some traditional Enochian scholars, but, as Crowley said, "When you use the Ouija board, you give permission for any unknown spirit to communicate with you. Would you open the front door to your house and let in anybody who felt like it? Of course not." The Watchtowers are critical because they provide control. Instead of the door opening and randomly asking, "Is anyone there?" they allow us to open a specific gate and to know exactly whom we're summoning and from where they come, long before we place our hands upon the planchette.

In the first chapter we mentioned that the ultimate secret behind the Ouija board is this control. If such control is lacking on any plane then what one obtains, especially through a Ouija board, is little more than a lucid window whereby uncontrolled imagery from the subconscious mind is allowed to stream forth. Success with the board can only be achieved if it is used in conjunction with ritualistic and ceremonial techniques of High Magick. This is why you must study and understand the Watchtowers.

The earliest vision wherein these Watchtowers appeared to Edward Kelly, the skryer with whom John Dee was working, was received in the early morning hours of Wednesday, June 20th, 1584. Dee writes that to Kelly appeared "four very fair castles, standing in the four parts of the world: out of which he heard the sound of a Trumpeter. Then seemed out of every Castle a cloath to be thrown on the ground, of more than the breadth of a Table-cloath. Out of that in the East, the cloath seemed to be red, which was cast. Out of that in the South, the cloath seemed white. Out of that in the West, the cloath seemed green, with knops on it. Out of that in the North, spread, or thrown out from the gate under foot, the cloath seemed to be very black."[1]

With time it would be realized that the term Castle and Watchtower were, in some respects, synonymous with each other. Another vision further elaborated the colors of these Castles, stating the eastern color is "red; after the new smitten blood," the south as "white, Lilly-colour," the west was, "the skins of many dragons, green: garlick-bladed" and toward the north the color of "bilbery juyce."[2] We mention these visions because in the numerous modern books on Enochian magick the elemental colors have changed; they are not what are found in Dee's original manuscripts.

It is believed that this variation in colors first appeared in the private grade papers of a British fraternity known as The Hermetic Order of the Golden Dawn, in which Aleister Crowley had been trained. It was done in order to reflect the more traditional astral or "western" elemental Flashing Colors. According to the Golden Dawn Grade Papers, when certain colors are placed side by side in opposition with their direct complementary color it creates a "flashing" tendency which automatically attracts elementals. Whether true or not, the validity of this color change has been hotly debated amongst Enochian scholars for years. Some believe the color change attracts only those elemental qualities inherent in lower astral currents, rather than the true angelic entities as seen by Dee in his visions, and is therefore limiting. These same scholars point out that mortals had no right to change the original colors as dictated by the angels; others disagree, claiming we mortals know better. Some have stated that the change simply came about to reflect what is known as the King Scale of colors from the Qabalistic Tree of Life. Regardless of why, most books on Enochian magick since the twentieth century give the color attributes differently than what John Dee and Edward Kelly originally saw.

These four castles are also referred to as four houses, which are "the 4 Angels of the Earth, which are the 4 Overseers, and Watch-towers" and in "each of these Houses, the Chief Watchman, is a mighty Prince, a mighty Angel of the Lord."[3] The term Watchtower not only implies a place where angelic sentinels are stationed to stand guard and protect God's Kingdom from the profane, but also it tells us that these Hidden Gates have a connection to the Watchers themselves, or those entities that descend and guide humanity like the Enochian angels when summoned appropriately. Often taken lightly by Enochian scholars is a wonderful vision of these Castle-like structures, which was disclosed to Edward Kelly in the form of a specific Holy Table standing on four legs. Kelly claims that the angel in his vision "spreadeth the aire, or openeth it before him, and there appeareth before a square Table."[4] On its top was a huge rectangle comprised of squares in rows of twenty-five across by twenty-seven down.

This concept of heaven as a table suspended over our earth is important in its similarities to other legends of heaven, especially those found in ancient Egypt. The Egyptians believed that heaven was shaped like a huge rectangle similar not only to the Holy Table of John Dee, but also to the shape of a Ouija board. This rectangular heaven was suspended over our earth by four pillars, each represented by a god. These lesser gods were actually the four children of the Sun God Horus. They were Kabexnuv, the hawk-headed mummy that rules the elemental quality of fire; Tmoumathph, the dog-headed mummy of water; Ahephi, the ape-headed mummy, which rules air; and Ameshet, the human-headed mummy, which rules the quality of earth.

In many ways these four pillars or table legs represent the four astral tides as they descend upon our earth. In all cases the central Sun is the source of the currents that bathe our planet. The Egyptians believed that one could petition a specific god for any given knowledge about the heavens and our Earth. His name was Ptah, which literally means the Opener. He was the grand architect who built the heavens and who knows all its hidden secrets. This concept of requesting knowledge from the Watchers, archangels or whomever in the Enochian system is comparable to the guidance given through a Ouija board. The similarities are striking.

At this point we must further examine the breakdown of John Dee's Holy Table. Many of the attributes which we now accept as being part of the Enochian system actually originated in the Hermetic Order of the Golden Dawn around the turn of the century. For example, we have come to learn that the central vertical line and the middle horizontal line of the Holy Table are attributed to "spirit" or Akasha. The Akasha is often equated as being a fifth element or solar tide, but this is misleading because it implies a similarity to the others. In fact, it is independent and invisible in relationship to the other four. Also, above the Akasha are two more Tattwas that actually bring the total to seven. These forces are known as the Anapadaka and the Adi Tattwas. We know that the lower five Tattwas work through and correspond with our five senses; the sixth and seventh are latent in humanity and are rarely activated. We are concerned here with that which encompasses our five senses in order to lay a suitable Foundation whereby possibilities exist to open one's sixth sense through a Ouija board.

As we've already stated, Vayu/Air/Smell, Apas/Water/Taste, Tejas/Fire/Sight and Prithivi/Earth/Touch are the four subtle currents encompassing all manifestations. In a metaphysical sense, those individuals who are bound up into Laws of these four are usually the slaves who will perish. (*Liber AL vel Legis* II:49) A Thelemite considers them to be damned, or forced to remain in an animalistic existence. The nature of the fifth sense, attributed to Spirit, is far loftier and encompasses the Akasha, which rules the sense of Hearing. It is in this fifth sense wherein lies the sacred child in Black Egg, and understanding its nature can bring us to the threshold of our sixth sense. (*Liber AL vel Legis* II:49) This is because Hearing is twofold. It acts as a bridge, and can be focused either toward the material plane or into the realm of the Spirit. Hearing is attributed to the Tarot card known as the Hierophant, which is ruled by the Hebrew letter of Vau, meaning nail. A nail is something that binds one thing to another. Vau is also the Hebrew conjunction "and" which unites sentences. This implies that the nature of the Akasha, as mimicked within the crosses, not only binds but divides the elemental qualities, regardless of where they might be found—from the mundane to the spiritual. In some ways a pain of division is left in its wake by the Akasha as four elemental sections. Each section is then a Watchtower or Castle on the Holy Table.

With this in mind we must understand the nature of the Holy Table. Each Watchtower has a defined hierarchy. The letters found on the central cross of the Holy Table, when written out in four rows of five letters each, together are known as The Tablet of Union. In its division it creates the four great Watchtowers. In the upper left quadrant of this Holy Table is the Watchtower that rules the elemental quality of air. It is attributed toward the direction of the rising sun or east; originally its color was that of red, like blood, but modern magicians have changed this to yellow. The right quadrant or Watchtower is ruled by Water and is attributed toward the west. Its color was formerly described as being like the skins of many dragons, or "green, garlick-bladed," but has been changed to blue, being more symbolic of water. The lower right side of the Holy Table is ruled by fire and is attributed toward the south. Its color now is red, where originally it was a "white, Lilly-color." Finally, the bottom left is ruled by earth and is attributed toward the north. Its color is the only one that remains the same (black), although it is also referred as being sort of bilberry-juice color in nature.

Each of the four Watchtowers is composed of twelve squares across and thirteen down, or 156 squares total. This numerically is the value of the word BABALON that is also known as The Gate of the Sun. The two center vertical lines and the middle horizontal line across each Watchtower forms what is known as The Grand Cross. These crosses are often shown as being white on a colored depiction of the Watchtowers. This denotes that these squares are of a spiritual Akashic nature rather than an elemental one. The horizontal lines of these crosses are very important because they contain the three Secret Holy Names of God ruling the elemental Sun of each Watchtower. In all there are twelve sacred names on the four Tablets that act as a bridge between the Macrocosm and the Microcosm. These names consist of the first three squares, the next four and the final five. On the Air Watchtower we get the names ORO, IBAH, AOZPI. For the Water Watchtower we get MPH, ARSL, GAIOL. For the Fire Watchtower we get OIP, TEAA, PDOCE, and finally, for the Earth Watchtower we get MOR, DIAL, HCTGA.

Equally important, just like our own Solar System, the center of The Grand Cross is attributed to the Sun that is ruled by a great Enochian King. The name of each King is extracted from a spiral whirl of eight squares found within the Central Cross on each Watchtower. There are four Elemental Kings in all, one in each Tablet. When a magician invokes the three Secret Holy Names of God, the King is automatically activated. It is through these eight central squares that all the universal and elemental forces emerge to animate the Watchtowers, similar to the way in which the tides themselves manifest our own Universe. The three Secret Holy Names of God, along with the King, must always be invoked whenever lower elemental forces on the Tablet are to be utilized.

The six points on the Grand Cross extending from the center of the board are attributed to the planets and our moon. These are vertically two lines on the top and two on the bottom, and then horizontally one line on either side. Starting with the top left vertical line and going clockwise, we have the line of Jupiter, Moon, Venus, Saturn, Mercury and Mars. Each line is ruled by what is termed a Senior. The Seniors are directly below the Holy King in the order of Hierarchy on a Watchtower. Since there are six Seniors on each Watchtower and four Watchtowers, there are twenty-four Seniors total. They are mentioned in The Book of Revelation as the twenty-four Elders who are clothed in white and who sit on the twenty-four thrones before God. These Seniors act as a conduit for the specific type of elemental force originating from a particular planet. and are automatically invoked with a King.

It becomes obvious that each Watchtower symbolically represents our universe, with planets swirling around a central Sun. It also mimics being suspended by four elemental legs similar to the rectangular structure of heaven according to the Egyptians. Since each Watchtower has a central Grand Cross, it too is divided into four equal quadrants, or legs, similar to the Holy Table itself. The attributes are the same, meaning that the upper left quadrant of each Watchtower is attributed to Air, the right Water, bottom right is Fire and the bottom left Earth. No elemental quality is ever pure. It must contain within itself the other three qualities on a lesser level in order to function properly. The same theory also pertains to the invisible solar tides or Tattwas known as Vayu, Tejas, Apas and Prithivi: although each is primarily attributed to one of the four elemental qualities of air, fire, water and earth, they must contain within themselves the other three to a lesser degree in order to manifest.

Within each of the four quadrants on a Watchtower is a Lesser Cross of ten squares that is often called a Sephirotic or Calvary Cross. These squares represent the sub-planetary elemental aspects of the universe. These crosses are shown as being white. Like the Grand Cross ruled by the planetary Seniors, this denotes that these Lesser Crosses are also of a spiritual or Akashic nature rather than an elemental one. Each cross contains the sacred names of two important Holy Angels. These two names are used when invoking a specific subservient angel or elemental in a quadrant. The descending line forms a six-lettered name that a magician uses to call forth anything from the Watchtower's quadrant, while the horizontal name of five letters is used to command and control that which has been summoned. These are the two names that must be memorized when working with an elemental through a Ouija board.

Directly above the arms of each cross are four squares, two on either side. These squares represent the Cherubics who are described as being four in number, each with four faces and with four wings. They are the ruling forces of the elemental within the quadrant directly under the authority of two Angels ruling the Lesser Cross. They represent the "fixed" signs of the Zodiac. The Cherubics are often equated with Archangels or, in particular, a class known as the Watchers. They are assigned to help regulate and balance any and all forces employed within the quadrant in its relationship to manifestation. Below the arms we have four rows of four descending squares or twelve squares each. These squares designate the realms of both angels and lower elementals. If one understands how to put four squares together with a fifth, by choosing one square from each horizontal row then one can summon a specific angel who is under the rulership of an Archangel. (*Liber AL vel Legis* II:49) If one opens one single solitary square of the twelve, then one can open a gateway by which a specific type of elemental can descend.

You must learn how to utilize these elemental squares first. It can be argued than an Adept should seek higher or loftier aspirations but one must learn to crawl before one can walk. Working a Ouija Board opens the astral floodgates onto Malkuth or our Earth, and when you make use of the board you will be attracting elementals automatically, whether you call them or not. Realizing this dilemma, if you must have familiar spirits in the lower astral plane who act as guides, then let them be servants that you have purposefully called forth and control.

CHAPTER SEVEN

"The hollow shells glow with infernal fire. Also, of course, they soak up vitality from the sitters, and from the medium herself."

—ALEISTER CROWLEY

S ome people have wondered if an elemental is really dangerous when it shape-shifts into our wildest dreams or fantasies. Although the answer may appear to be obvious, there are other subtle pitfalls not readily known outside magick. For instance, the more a person communicates with an elemental the stronger *it* becomes. It gains its strength by feeding on your life-energy. This relationship is properly or magickally called a marriage—more precisely, a *Lesser Marriage*. You must never forget that Yesod or the Moon on the Qabalistic Tree of Life rules the astral realm inhabited by these entities. It has absolutely no natural source of illumination. When you read or hear the term astral *light* it is a misnomer. This realm is not composed of light in any sense that the average person may comprehend; it is actually bathed in a darkness of the blackest kind. Since humans are naturally solar beings, when we immerse ourselves into the astral our Light, or life-source, illuminates the realm and gives it purpose as dictated by our *thoughts*. Like the Moon itself, the only source of illumination for this realm and its inhabitants is a Sun. "Every man and every woman is a star"—in other words, as soon as our Sun illuminates the darkness it attracts elementals like moths to the light. In turn they feed on this Light. It animates them.

All of this is typical magickal rhetoric, but what does it mean for someone wishing to work with elementals through a Ouija board? Let us examine the casual statement above regarding feeding: Aleister Crowley knew of this danger when summoning elementals or the Qliphoth Shells of the Dead. Besides being very obsessive creatures desiring to attach themselves to mortals, Crowley wrote that these "hollow shells glow with infernal fire. Also, of course, they soak up vitality from the sitters, and from the medium herself."[1] This warning must be heeded carefully if one wishes to communicate with Shells or elementals on a continual basis. An elemental *must* be fed, and if not from your own psyche, then from something else.

The author of *The Exorcist*, William Blatty, who deeply researched the supernatural for his book, also understood this elemental requirement: "A demon wants the kick of being married to a human nervous system. Like Henry the Eighth wanting to eat a thirty-course meal again."[2] Although I don't agree with him on the term "demon," I concur in regard to feeding on a human nervous system. Every Medium will attest to the fact that after communicating with the spirit world they become very tired or drained. Where did their energy go? Energy cannot dissipate; it has to go somewhere even if it is absorbed by an invisible entity. When I once asked a similar question of my own teacher, he said, "Look, I eat, you eat and they eat—what's the problem?" I thought about it and replied, "I guess there is no problem." Elementals, like all of God's creatures, need nourishment to survive, otherwise they die and fade away.

However, to explain further the dangers of allowing the entity to use *you* as the source of its feeding, let's look at another simple analogy. If your psyche or nervous system were similar to twenty-two-gauge wire, how much current could you draw before the wires burned out? Could it draw 100 amps? Of course not—a burnout would be inevitable, resulting in a serious fire. Without careful training to become a vehicle through magick, yoga, or similar methods, most psychic systems will be ill-prepared for any influx or surge of life-current. This solar energy animates us. Its strength is in relationship to its ability to flow through our psychic system unhampered. The greater the system, the more current it can take.

On the other hand, an elemental must feed, and by feeding it draws off your life (solar) energy at an alarming rate. We cannot say how long it will take since every individual is different, but, sooner or later, your psychic "wires" will begin to get hot and this elemental, a parasite by nature, doesn't know when to stop. Its thirst, like a baby suckling its mother, is insatiable when a host is found. Unfortunately, just like a circuit breaker, when the wires start to get too hot something has to pop, usually with disastrous psychic or mental ramifications in the case of a human being. This is why all invisible beings, good or bad, must be controlled and not allowed to venture further at their discretion.

Once again it is important for me to assert that elementals are not evil by nature. They are simply fulfilling their needs as any creature would, visible or invisible. Armed with common sense, you must learn how to feed them. As an example, if you do not feed your cat or dog, what would it do? It would roam in quest for food. But most people who unleash an elemental through a Ouija board do not realize that it, too, will roam your home in search of a host, or food. Again, this does not imply the elemental is evil; rather, it is just fulfilling its nature like all creatures that require nourishment.

The elemental is not the only creature that feeds off our anatomy. Microscopic bugs, parasites and germs live on everything from our eyelashes to our skin, but these are accepted as merely part of nature. The elemental is similarly parasitical but, like lions, tigers and bears, the ramifications of its feeding can often be disastrous where a human is concerned. Whether one loses body or psyche to any "feeder," visible or invisible, is not a reality one wishes to embrace.

Everyone should learn the nature of elementals before they intend to work with them. Failure to fully understand and take precautions can produce solemn consequences. If you doubt that this could occur to you, then you should read about hauntings originating through a Ouija board: you'll quickly uncover hundreds of stories about people who have become possessed, drained and pushed to the edge of a mental or psychic breakdown. Usually this is a child or the youngest person in a household, or an unstable adult. The choice of feeding off the youngest person by an elemental, although seemingly baneful, is simply because of the nature of a human's psychic system. The older a person gets, the harder it is to open that which time has begun to close down; we become earth-bound with age. This in itself would take an entire volume to explain adequately, but, essentially, the more earth-bound or wrapped in Maya we become, the more destined we are toward an earthly grave. Most children, on the other hand, are simply "open" for anything. Magicians must learn to be like children.

If you're worried about this concept of feeding, let me point out that it's quite easy to eliminate the danger of becoming an elemental's host. When continually evoking elementals through the Ouija board, you should simply consider alternative forms of food, rather than yourself or others. Like any life force, the elemental gains in strength and can communicate clearer when it's fed. It gives in relationship to its ability, and that ability is determined by how strong it becomes. The relationship being fostered between you and an elemental is symbiotic and similar to other relationships that are forged in nature. We use them and they, in turn, require something from us; we cannot take, take, take, and then give nothing in return.

Feeding spirits is something not limited to Ouija board

workings. Within Aleister Crowley's *De Nuptiis Secretis, Deorum cum Hominibus* (literally translated as the *Secret Marriages of the Gods with Men*) there are certain methods mentioned which point out the need to strengthen the elemental by feeding it a certain substance within a pyramid. Many cultures and religions throughout the world realize the importance of feeding or making offerings to the spirit world. The easiest way to achieve this is to place flowers, food or drink, or even sexual fluids on a specially prepared altar, which is used as a focal point in the ceremonies. Some voodoo rituals or similar methods should be carefully studied as they give excellent examples on how this can be achieved. If one wonders how an elemental distinguishes between you and the altar, it's quite simple: like a cat or dog, it feeds where it is trained. However, if you don't put food in its bowl then it will hunt elsewhere, just like any creature—a fact that you must never forget. The type of offering that you make is usually determined by the type of elemental you've decided to work with. Since we know there are four distinct types of elementals ruling fire, earth, air and water, it is easy to figure out the type of offering in relationship to the qualities of the elemental.

The altar itself should simply be a designated spot where only things pertinent to the elemental are placed. Nothing else should ever grace this location. It could be a small wooden table placed in the corner of a room, a shelf attached to a wall, or a corner of the floor. Your imagination is the limit, and there is no right or wrong place. If in doubt, ask the elemental itself if such and such an item can be added to the altar or if an existing decoration is pleasing. Elementals simply love any attention they get and anything you suggest is usually accepted by them. In some ways it's like a child being given a new toy: rarely is it ever turned down.

It is important to note that if anybody else ever touches these items on the altar it should be considered a sacrilege. Only you, or those directly involved with the ritual workings, should touch items on the altar. Anyone else will break the Magickal Link and the elemental could attach itself to the individual's psyche with disastrous results. The altar is sacred. Defend it. Let no heathen defile it.

Although the entire altar can be dedicated to the elemental, the food or offering should always be placed within a pyramid. This term can be misleading because it implies an actual structure rather than a flat drawn-out triangular object. In *De Nuptiis Secretis, Deorum cum Hominibus* it tells us that our offering must "be preserved within the pyramid of the letters that make up the name of the spirit." In addition to writing the name in the triangle, the offering should be restricted only within this symbol, whether it is flowers, or a dish of food, water, incense or whatever. The elemental will quickly learn that this is its feeding spot. You should never banish or cleanse this location. You'll want this location to become a strong Magickal Link between this world and the elemental. With time it will become apparent.

Some people have voiced a strong concern about the elemental breaking his tethers and roaming the house because you're giving him an open doorway via the altar, or triangle. Rest assured there are always added precautions that can be taken if you're worried. For one, elementals cannot cross a circle of salt placed around the triangle. This is the one substance that will bind the elemental within a given area on our plane. In studying the arts of alchemy we learn that salt fixes or solidifies and restricts that which we want contained.

The magical implement that corresponds symbolically to salt is the magician's chain, and it can also bind an elemental in the same way that salt does. Simply place the chain in a circular fashion around your triangle. An elemental cannot cross it. Although often misunderstood or omitted from many people's magickal arsenal, you must obtain this implement. Furthermore, it is important that the chain contains exactly 333 links.

Aleister Crowley writes that "The Chain is Salt: it serves to bind the wandering thoughts; and for this reason is placed about the neck of the Magician."[3] This quote refers to how a magician can deal with his wandering mind during rituals, rather than external elemental workings. However, in the case where one cannot focus their thoughts during the Ouija working, such can be employed as Crowley specifies. On an elemental level, by placing the chain in a circular fashion around the triangle, it will bind the entity within the image. If you're still unclear on how this works, simply do it for now, even if for no other reason than to dedicate the chain as a sacred object on your altar.

The symbolism behind 333 links is that it represents the sacred numeration of an entity known as Choronzon. Magicians strongly believe that this demon is as real as day and night, although a contradiction in his being implies that he doesn't exist in the same sense as we exist. He lives in the realm of a vast astral desert known as the Abyss between the Pylons of Daath, or Knowledge. Some refer to him as the Guardian of all Shells, for he guards reality from the known and the unknown. He knows the Truth or has the Knowledge behind every person's illusions or life. This is why he is often called the Lord of Chaos and Dispersion. He brings everything to light and exposes our folly, which is something few mortals want thrown in their face, especially those climbing the sacred mountain of Abiegnus toward spiritual heights.

However, just beyond the Abyss is the realm known as Binah on the Qabalistic Tree of Life. Binah is ruled by the attributes of Saturn. Crowley notes that one of the magical weapons of Saturn is the Sickle and that such can "be used in actual ceremony to threaten the spirit that Choronzon will cut short his independent existence"[4] if he does not submit to one's demands. The Sickle, like the chain and salt, can be used as a weapon against the spirit or elemental. Simply inform it that if it doesn't oblige your wishes, "Choronzon will reap his

Karma, and add it to the treasure of Choronzon's storehouse."[5] No elemental can withstand the threat of being taken by Choronzon!

Few mortals who truly understand the nature of this demon will likewise go against him unprepared. We have already spoken of the inherent dangers of using a Ouija board and how one can lose all while playing in the astral realms. Crowley warns that the biggest threat is the loss of one's Karma, or the "Surrender of the Soul to Choronzon."[6] This implies that your whole existence, the very nature of the experience for which your Spirit has incarnated, has been dragged into the depths of dispersion and chaos. Remember, it's written that all of your emotions, thoughts and experiences make up the constitution of your Shell. Everything is recorded upon this Shell as if it were a video or a movie. How tragic it would be if the experiences you were going through were composed only of madness or intellectual befuddlement caused by following false gods or concepts made by the feeble imaginations of others, as well as yourself. Such falsities and beliefs are tied to your spirit's karma for all eternity. Be careful—it *is* possible to lose your soul, and it is Choronzon who will expose these follies to you if you attempt to reach his lair by seeking the Knowledge of the Shells under his domain, especially those relating to your own Shell.

How this relates to an elemental is simple. These entities exist in a pliable dreamscape of archetypal symbolism. They crave human experiences, and activating Shells help them achieve this. To them, they're incarnating into a higher being, if only for a moment in time. To lose this ability terrifies the elemental and the threat of Choronzon is something very real, especially if the vehicle you've given them is based upon falsities.

Here I must offer a little fatherly advice. Although you can threaten the elemental with Choronzon as if it were the bogeyman, avoid doing such while working the Ouija board.

You should always be kind to the elemental and treat it like you would your own child. Never abuse it or treat it in a condescending manner. It needs your guidance, just as a child would, and you must learn to be its parent. If abused, an elemental can turn on you and mimic that which has been done to it. Remember Crowley's warning that the astral world is like a mirror. Be careful what you project into the elemental kingdom. Threats given can be threats received. The difference between control and abuse is a fine line on all planes.

Since I have brought up some Qabalistic theory with such terms as the Abyss and the Pylons of Daath or Knowledge, I think it best to elaborate as to how this information further unfolds the mysteries of how a Ouija works. First, I'd like you to consider these verses from Proverbs:

> 19. The Lord of Wisdom hath founded the earth; and by his understanding hath he established the heavens.
> 20. By his knowledge the depths are broken up, and the clouds drop down the dew.

These two verses are so profound that an entire chapter could be written upon the Qabalistic thought and theory in regard to the Tree of Life and its ten spheres or Sephiroths. Essentially, they are an allegory for how two Qabalistic Spheres unite to produce a third. In verse 19, "Wisdom" refers to the second Qabalistic sphere known as Chokmah. "Understanding" is the third sphere of Binah. These are the eternal male[2] and female[3] qualities. They are also equated in our own psyche with the Chiah (animus +) and Neschamah (anima -). Once united, they bring into play a third sphere, which is beyond the ten and actually forms an eleventh sphere normally hidden and invisible on the Tree of Life. This sphere is known as Daath, a Hebrew word meaning Knowledge as mentioned in verse 20. This implies that the father and mother unite to produce a child.

To achieve this, Chokmah and Binah are united by a horizontal path ruled by the Hebrew letter Daleth on the Tree of Life which when translated means a door. Once this door is opened, the influence from above (Kether) descends downward through the Qabalistic path known as Gimel, or the High Priestess. This path represents receptivity, or, according to Qabalists, it is the uniting intelligence within the subconscious. The path of Gimel further descends into Tiphereth, the sixth Qabalistic Sphere ruling our Sun. It then moves through our Sun using the solar tides or Tattwas to descend into our world.

The Qabalistic realm known as the Qliphoth, briefly mentioned earlier, is generally considered to be an evil realm by both Qabalists and ceremonial magicians alike, although many are beginning to realize that this is simply dogma fostered by religious fearmongers of the past Aeon and carried through into modern times. For every positive current there is a negative current, but the Qliphoth is generally not evil in relationship to the Tree of Life so much as a negative relationship to our reality. The Qliphoth is said to be the realm filled with the lingering Shells of people's thoughts, either dead or alive. Contacting this realm is what we've been discussing throughout this book. In some respects the dangers can be very real to a novice working with a Ouija board, but should we avoid these forces? Absolutely not. Even the most Sacred Magic of Abramelin the Mage, which teaches humanity how to find their Holy Guardian Angel, states that through a prolonged period of purification and preparation the aspirant must call forth angelic forces as well as demonic to balance his spiritual attainment, in order that his angel might descend. You must learn to work with both Yesed (Moon) and Tiphereth (Sun).

All these Qabalistic theories imply is that two people are required to work a Ouija board by ritualistic methods. The two who are working the planchette should be of opposite sex, to represent the eternal male and female qualities of Chokmah and Binah. In their union of touching hands on the planchette, the astral light stirs and an influence descends through the fourfold door, symbolized by the shape of the board itself. The influence is then bound within the triangle, or planchette. The board is a fourfold door that represents Daleth, while the triangle or three-sided figure equates to Gimel. These are the two paths whereby the hidden influence of Knowledge (Daath) is allowed to descend the Tree of Life into our Sun and then through it. The sacred child (elemental) who has been brought through the door then communicates with the person who represents this solar quality, and it is through him that the entity will act and move determined by the questions he asks.

The researcher Hester Travers Smith elaborated the same principle about the two people working the board. She wrote, "At the ouija-board, where two persons work together, it is all-important to discover mediums whose respective qualities balance and assist each other. The control (i.e. triangle) will generally say he requires 'a negative and a positive.' What this means exactly it is hard to understand, but from watching many combinations at the ouija-board I have gathered that a 'positive' medium receives the message through his or her brain and transmits it to the board, while a 'negative' possesses the driving force—I mean that, apparently, one sitter supplies mental, and the other muscular power."[7] This is an interesting concept, especially when reflecting upon Binah and Chokmah. She also pointed out: "Curiously enough I find sex is a factor in the choice of sitters. The best combination for ouija-work is a man and a woman. Two women sometimes work excellently together, but I have never come across an instance of any results worth speaking of being achieved by two men."[8] This might have been the case amongst her own circle of mediums, but I don't necessarily agree that two men cannot work the board. If two males are used then the quality of positive and negative personalities should be obvious, but I do agree that, on average, two males tend to "earth" out the board.

On another metaphysical level, the same philosophy which gives us the most intricate theories behind the Tattwas tells us that these tides came into play when two eternal forces of male and female, known as Siva and Sakti, became united, similar to Chokmah and Binah. It is their twin essences of Prana (+) and Akasha (-) which are the underlying qualities of each tide. On one level, Prana is the four elemental forces while Akasha is considered to be the binding factor, often equated with the spirit, and the spirit itself encompasses all and beyond; it is not any one part of the given whole. The Akasha, on the other hand, is also called the etheric currents or astral light, which equates closely with the qualities of the soul. Qabalists claim this comes into play in the ninth Sephiroth of Yesed, which is attributed to the Moon, for the Moon reflects the Sun's light and the currents that emanate from it. The path on the Tree of Life that is ruled by the Moon is Gimel, which allows the influences to descend from Daath and above.

Although this chapter might be possibly hard to grasp thus far without a good foundation in magickal or Qabalistic theory, Aleister Crowley said it best when he wrote that he has "spoken of the Sephiroth, and the Paths, of Spirits and Conjurations; of Gods, Spheres, Planes, and many other things which may or may not exist. It is immaterial whether they exist or not. By doing certain things certain results follow."[9] We cannot always have concrete evidence at our fingertips to prove or disprove any given theory, but if one follows the directions of others and duplicates their experiments, the results should be identical. When adding 1 + 1 you should always get 2, and the same is true for magickal rituals.

Let's return to the subject of feeding, as there are still a few things to discuss before ending this chapter. If you're confused and don't know exactly what to offer upon your altar, you could simply ask the elemental. He will usually tell you of the type of offering required which is most suitable for him. As a rule, if the elemental requests any form of blood as an offering, decline to cooperate. Demand a substitute. Blood of any kind is unacceptable.

While a treatise of this nature cannot suitably explain in depth the serious dangers of a novice using blood, essentially you don't want the elemental to get a thirst for something so precious to yourself. If the elemental demands that his requests be met, remember that you are in charge, not him. If he still insists and refuses to give you a substitute other than blood, then banish him back into his domain, close the ritual down and start completely over on another evening in quest of a new elemental. Remember, most elementals are completely gracious and long for the opportunity to serve. Although rare, a demanding elemental is a dangerous elemental; if he is taking charge at the beginning, then you've got problems on the horizon, because he's fulfilling something twisted in your subconscious. Most elementals actually have wants as much as we do, but usually when shown who is in charge they will back down and comply with your demands. So before you befuddle your mind as to what to offer, ask the elemental what he'd like. This is the first step.

One thing that also needs to be clarified: feeding does not mean that the elemental will chomp away on your offering in the same fashion as we eat food. You don't have to worry about a little critter sitting around your apartment devouring the food and leaving little elemental turds in the corner. The elemental will drain the subtle life energy out of your offering and leave only the husk, or shell, of the original item on your altar. To the skeptic it may appear that the food simply decayed, but there are subtle differences between food rotting and something being drained of its life essence. These remnants of decayed matter are similar to the waste products produced by most animals, humans included; this rotting by-product should be thrown away and the altar replenished with a fresh offering.

How often you should change the offering is up to the

elemental. He will cry out into your subconscious and you will know when it's required to be changed. Don't wait until it decays to the point of mush; listen to your inner voice. It's like feeding any pet. You shouldn't have to be told—you should know when he needs to eat. Finally, no two elementals are alike in their feeding habits. You must learn your elemental's needs.

This should give you enough food for thought (no pun intended) to make you wary, cautious, and hopefully aware that Ouija is not a cute game, but real and dangerous to an untrained person. It takes years of researching and experimenting. It is said that a thousand people can play the board without a serious problem, but there is always that one time when a door is opened wider and a bridge is created between worlds. I argue that this is success.

CHAPTER EIGHT

*"To do magick without a record is like
trying to run a business without book-keeping."*

—ALEISTER CROWLEY

Carlos Castaneda was a Peruvian who studied anthropology at the University of California in Los Angeles. His special interest was medicinal plants. His first three books, *The Teachings of Don Juan*, *A Separate Reality* and *Journey to Ixtlan* (the last of which earned him his Ph.D.) have become best-selling counter-culture classics. In these books don Juan teaches Castaneda about what he calls the invisible "ally." This ally, like the witch's familiar, is exactly what the magician refers to as an elemental.

Castaneda's journey began along the Arizona/Mexico border in the summer of 1960, when he met a Yaqui Indian named don Juan Matus who claimed to be a *brujo* or sorcerer possessing "secret knowledge." It was under don Juan's guidance that Castaneda began an arduous apprenticeship that led him down a spiritual road to find himself, his power and his invisible ally. He achieved his goals through the use of drugs.

In our case, instead of "seeing between the worlds," we are attempting to communicate with our ally through a Ouija board. In both cases the magician is warned that they must never drop their guard or believe in everything they hear and see. For instance, don Juan told Castaneda that once you have found your ally you must *wrestle with it and tame it*, and that if you do not *control* your ally his "force" will torment you and you will be unable to shake it the rest of your life. We have already warned in previous chapters of obsessions and possessions, or creating hauntings and releasing terrifying poltergeists when you unleash the elemental rather than controlling it.

Let us further examine controlling the elemental in Aleister Crowley's *De Nuptiis Secretis, Deorum cum Hominibus*. Certain sections in this manuscript address in the Western tradition magickally what don Juan Matus was trying to teach Carlos Castaneda to achieve through a more shamanistic approach. Although issued publicly many times since it first appeared in print in 1914, it is now considered a secret Eighth Degree Grade Paper within the Ordo Templi Orientis and is hard to find.

In its section XI there is mention of the *Lesser Marriage*. Crowley tells the Adept that achieving a Lesser Marriage with these entities, or familiar spirits, is fairly easy, "for the souls of the elements desire constantly this salvation."[1] The inherent quality of an elemental hungers to be drawn into our life-cycle in order to elevate its own nature through redemption with the experience culminating in death, similar to why our own Divine Spirit incarnates.

Crowley further says that of all the familiar spirits, the "Spirits of the Elemental Tablets given by Dr. Dee and Sir Edward Kelly are the best, being very perfect in their nature and faithful, affectioning the human race," then gives the Adept certain warnings when bringing forth such beings, similar to what don Juan tells Carlos Castaneda. First Crowley tells us that we must wisely choose a specific elemental which has a "reasonable soul, docile, apt, beautiful, and in all ways worthy of love." This may seem like an almost impossible task, but it's actually quite simple: the elemental will always shape-shift into the image imposed upon it by the magician. When

Crowley warns us to choose the familiar spirit's garments well, he is telling us to be aware that the types of questions we ask through a Ouija board serve to mold or clothe the elemental.

Secondly, the Adept should never forget the Greater Marriage. In basic terms, if you're going to work with elementals, you must also seek your Holy Guardian Angel. Everyone has an Angel assigned to them at birth. A simple prayer where you request your Angel's guidance is all that is required in Ouija workings. After all, the realm of the Angels is that of the Sun and inevitably the source of the Laws of Abrac to which we are all aspiring. John Dee and Edward Kelly always began their workings with intense prayers. After they had fulfilled their affirmations, they simply set themselves before a table and began skrying into the crystal. When working the Ouija board one should take heed of the simplistic methods in which Dee and Kelly achieved their communications. Without some sort of guidance from your Angel you are in danger of becoming a pawn to your own Malkuthian desires through the board, and you could easily attract an evil spirit.

The third warning which Crowley gives to the Adept is that "of such familiar spirits he have but four," one from each element. The magician should determine which one will be summoned and when; you "regulate their service, appointing hours for each." It is very important to be astrally balanced in the four elements but there is no way to determine exactly how long it will take to achieve this because no two individuals are alike. It may take a lifetime, partially due to the fact that you do not invoke all four elementals at once, but rather in a specific order over a period of time.

You always begin with the first elemental force, or Prithivi, which is Earth. It is the easiest force to master and offers the least amount of problems if it becomes untethered. Remember that each elemental force carries within itself the qualities of the other three; for example, Earth or Prithivi is not 100% Earth, but the quality of Earth is strongest in this particular tide or Tattwa in which an Elemental of Earth moves. The next strongest quality *within* Earth is that of Water, then Fire and finally Air. These four aspects, in the order just mentioned, must be invoked and controlled one by one before you can consider yourself a true master of the Earth (Prithivi) element in general. To work a Ouija board safely, you should have four different elementals under the rulership of the element of Earth which will stand before the four corners of your Universe to guide and protect you. You must learn to regulate their hours and their days as to when you communicate with them.

Crowley and others believe that these four elementals are all that are required for a suitable and balanced astral foundation. These four are quite sufficient for most Ouija workings, and once they have been drawn into harmony they give the ability to communicate through a Ouija board with the next or higher form of beings known as the Angels. In effect, by learning to control elementals you're laying an astral, or Lunar, foundation for the Laws of Abrac.

Finally, Crowley warns the Adept that he must treat his elemental "with kindness and firmness, being on guard against their tricks." As already stated, to bring forth an elemental comes with dire warnings. In theory, they do not exist in the astral until we bring them to birth, and in doing such you are creating a new order of beings. You must never forget your role in their development as their father or mother. In the mundane world parents look at their children and wish the best for them; they try to teach their child well, grooming and preparing him or her to take an active role in society. Magicians must raise their elemental the same way. We teach them by the types of questions we ask and we groom them to fulfill our needs.

There are some rudimentary requirements for using a Ouija board effectively. One of these prerequisites is to keep a Magickal Record of your working. This important requirement is different from a Magickal Diary in that the diary contains the record of a magician's daily life as a means of understanding self in relationship to why they incarnated. A Magickal Record is the account of a specific magickal working which has a set beginning and an end. If a person fails to keep a record when using a Ouija board they border on dangerous waters. Like every magickal exercise, the theory behind this practice is simple but multi-layered to include intricate reasons for the advanced student. In a Ouija ritual you must undertake the serious responsibility of acting like a scientist, and if a scientist does not keep a careful record to show how they achieved their results then their "experiments" are never taken seriously. Likewise, an individual who does not keep a Magickal Record of their Ouija workings, then claims an accomplishment and has no record to show for it, is suspect of deceit. You must verify the first step in your journey, the second and so forth that led you to a conclusion. Aleister Crowley tells us that the first and absolutely essential task for all his students is to keep a Magickal Record. He gives no exceptions to this rule.

Even if you have absolutely no plans to make public your workings, and what you are doing is solely for your own personal reasons between yourself and your elementals, you must still keep a Magickal Record. In fact, it is more important that you realize you're keeping the record not for others but for yourself. When beginning any Ouija ritual, you should consider yourself a pathfinder who is sailing off into uncharted waters: the realm of the astral. This is no child's game. You need maps, and the only way to obtain such is to draw them up yourself as you go along. Regarding this need for "maps and records" Crowley wrote, "Without this you are in the position of a navigator with neither chart nor log."[2]

If you did a one-night ritual and kept a bleak record, it offers you no way to adequately determine the results of your venture. If you were to continue night after night on a Ouija board, careful and intricate records are required to enable you to determine whether or not you are in dangerous territory and being led astray by lying spirits. To continue forward you must always reflect upon past communications and the steps that you've already taken. If you do not study the previous entries in your Magickal Record before each new venture, you could miss a valuable clue which, left unchecked, could release the elemental from its tethers or lead you off into some unconscious meaningless fantasy. If problems are apparent in your records, study them and determine what is required to overcome them; if things work well, obviously you've planned things correctly. Therefore, duplicate your successes and go further. You are a scientist and magick is no toy.

Let's review the Magickal Record more in depth. In addition to the date, your entry should also list the Sun sign, as well as the zodiac sign in which the Moon is at the time of the working. Even though you'll begin working with an Earth elemental, the Sun Sign pervades this elemental's quality once it manifests through a Ouija board, similar to how one's own astrological chart and personality is affected daily. You will definitely want to work with your earth elemental under a Sun sign with which you are compatible rather than one antagonistic toward your own. Any good book on astrology will tell you which signs work best with you. As an example, if you were born a Cancer then some of the signs best suited for you are Scorpio, Pisces, Taurus and Virgo. The rest are more neutral except for two: Aries and Libra. These could prove to be very difficult. With Capricorn, being the polar opposite of your Sun sign, there could be a great attraction toward it along with tension.

What happens if a person born under the sign of Cancer enthusiastically wanted to start working the Ouija board on, say, April 9th under the Sun sign of Aries, and they simply could not wait for a more appropriate astrological sign to be on the horizon? All you can say to such a person is "Go ahead." First, study Aries traits, and then be sure to keep a careful record. If the elemental becomes problematic you know why. Be this as it may, all signs technically get along, but knowing the Sun sign in which you're working gives you an edge into understanding how the elemental's personality is manifesting.

When I mention "manifested qualities" I must remind you that, unlike yourself, the elemental does not have a body. Astrologically, laws dictated by our Sun sign as it creates a body or the Maya, through which our Spirit will experience its incarnation, rule us. Besides the elemental's personality, the Sun sign also determines the type of manifestation that occurs when it extends its powers into our world. According to *The Sacred Magic of Abramelin the Mage*, although referred to in this book as demons, these elementals created all things in the world and they use the fourfold elemental building-blocks of our Universe to do such. They create simply by manifesting.

If one were working with a strong Earth elemental while the Sun and Moon were in Earth signs, with favorable timing and other aspects all lined up like an Earth slot machine, one can only imagine what might occur upon this plane if that elemental extended his abilities outward into our world. In my Temple in Connecticut I once worked with Water elementals for a lengthy period and experienced what some magicians might term a "blowout." The elemental slipped its tethers. Assistants working with me, and those who lived at our house, can tell horror stories about the plumbing, the roof leaking buckets, the sink and toilet flooding without reason. Manifestations occurred even on the most simple levels; however, these stopped abruptly when the ritual working was ended.

In the case of Earth elementals, who are the easiest to work with, the manifested characteristics are often seen as poltergeist type of bumps, thumps and rattlings around an apartment. Airy elementals often produce cold spots and unexplained drafts. You can now understand why all beginners are warned against using Fire elementals. If there is a "blowout" and manifestations begin to occur, it is important to determine how to banish the elemental. Naturally, if you are hearing bumps and thumps you wouldn't use a Fire Banishing Ritual; if you had been keeping good records you can determine quickly the type of ritual that must be used. Also, it is important to realize that just because you intended to evoke an Earth elemental doesn't mean you've gotten one automatically. It all depends on how intricately you planned and conducted the ritual itself.

Once an elemental begins "talking" through the board you'll have a manifested record to review. Another astrological aspect to consider is the Moon sign, because it reflects the characteristic nature of the elemental, as well as its creative and imaginative qualities, while it remains unmanifested and floating in the tides within the triangle. Naturally if you're a Cancer, an elemental that is manifesting under an Aries lunar tide might rub you wrong by the way it communicates. The Sun and Moon sign will help to determine how to analyze the communications that you have received from the elemental. While working any lengthy communication with a Ouija board, be sure to continually jot down the time when something out of the ordinary occurs in your surroundings. Later you may realize that the lunar qualities shifted drastically in the given moment, affecting the communication and creating the disturbance.

Another requirement is recording in the Magickal Record the astrological charts of everyone present during your ritual. You may find that certain people working with the triangle, or who are simply present, are incompatible with the elemental. You could also determine if an elemental is likely to attach itself to an individual with whom it feels more compatible— just like us mortals, the elemental will "click" with some people and not others. Also, the two people working the planchette represent the father and the mother. Their astrological qualities play an important role as to how the "child" or elemental will communicate and grow over a period of time. You want "parents" who will be suitable for raising a certain elemental born under a given astrological sign.

Besides the obvious reasons for keeping a Magickal Record, Aleister Crowley points out that "there are very great difficulties to be overcome in the training of the mind. Perhaps the greatest is forgetfulness, which is probably the worst form of what the Buddhists call ignorance. Special practices for training the memory may be of some use as a preliminary for persons whose memory is naturally poor. In any case the Magical Record ... is useful and necessary."[3] The average person lacks perfect recollection; often some memories about a given incident fade into obscurity. In working a Ouija board and communicating with elementals, the necessity for keeping such a record is apparent. You must know what the elemental had previously said in case contradictions slip into the communications. Remember, the elemental by nature is a lying spirit and learns this trait from you; it's not inherent in his being. Therefore, if contradictions appear, you must have a previous record to determine what might have inspired the elemental's answer. However, an elemental, when confronted with the multiplication of lies, will always tell the truth. I highly suggest that in addition to the two people working the triangle and a third asking questions, you employ a fourth who acts solely as the scribe to record everything that is occurring as well as the time. This being his only task, he can focus his mind more intensively on the Magickal Record.

Even the psychic Hester Travers Smith realized the importance of having a third person when experimenting with a Ouija board. She wrote, "In our own circle the words come through so quickly that it is almost impossible to read them, and it requires an experienced shorthand-writer to take them down when the traveller moves at its maximum speed."[4] Further: "Great care, accuracy, and rapidity are necessary to read the ouija-board, and this office should be taken entirely off the sitters' shoulders."[5] I agree—definitely employ a scribe.

If you decide to enter the communications into your computer diary, everything which was written down during a ritual by the scribe must be included; leave nothing out. Comment, don't edit. A good scientist doesn't edit anything but simply elaborates or footnotes upon what has been achieved. Everyone should make a point of reading these records and adding in their own comments or impressions. Again, leave nothing out. At no given time should the Record be closed to only one person's viewing. Also, never lie in your records: tell the good with the bad, cry into your soul with your failures, and elaborate upon your successes. If you begin telling lies, then what has the father taught his child, or the elemental?

It is crucial that you review the Magickal Record of the elemental working often. Don't just put in your daily entries and then put it aside; like a true scientist you should always look over the previous evening's workings before beginning any new venture. I suggest meeting with everyone before the next ritual to discuss the previous working, recording of course all new or pertinent comments. Not only will this help you remember what has been previously established, but it will also give indications as to what should be asked next. Plot a course of questions on your map but do not be rigid. Be flexible as to what you'll be asking. It is in an elemental's nature that they often drop a bombshell that you hadn't considered, and you may want to pursue what he had communicated. In this case it is OK to shift from the course plotted; after all, the main reason for doing any working is to establish a strong link between your world and his. If he is comfortable with talking, don't shut him up. However, do not blindly believe everything he's told you. Test him constantly.

I cannot stress enough: by his nature he is a lying spirit, but don't hate him or consider him evil for this quality. He'll only lie when trying to please the parents that brought him to birth. He achieves this by reading something in your subconscious that might be unbalanced. This is why the tides must flow evenly like a stream unhampered in your psyche. The people within the ritual should have no impressions in their subconscious waters regarding what should or should not be expected after a question is given. By keeping their minds and aspirations blank, the elemental can only respond with Truth. It is difficult to train people to concentrate on the question rather than an answer they'd like to hear, but this must be achieved.

If you find an elemental is lying far too much, it is advisable to ask him why, but do not become obsessed with determining the reason. The grave danger in this is that it may only encourage him. Your question should simply be directed toward discovering whom in the ritual chamber the elemental is trying to please by giving false answers. That is all. Be sure to demand the truth from the elemental if he is pointing the finger at someone in the ritual. If the elemental is already trying to please someone, he may pick up an unconscious thought from that given person that he or she may not want to be exposed, and therefore it will falsely finger someone else. (I've personally seen this happen; it's rather funny.) Again, test all communications for truth. If you find out that someone is unconsciously affecting the ritual you have only a few alternatives. The person should reflect deeply upon what they're unconsciously bringing into the ritual as determined by the false answers that the elemental has given. If they are in denial that it is them, or they cannot figure out what is unbalanced to enable themselves to right this wrong, they should no longer be allowed in the ritual chamber even as a spectator.

It has been asked whether it is OK to use a tape recorder. To this I say yes, but only one that uses batteries. This will be explained later. However, I would still recommend using a scribe. Part of his duty, which a recorder cannot achieve, is to write down the time when strange things occur, from temperature changes, thumps and bangs, to anything out of the ordinary. A tape recorder is a fantastic tool to accurately fill in the gaps of the evening's events and has even been known to pick up things that are not audible to the human ear, but it lacks something that only a scribe with eyes and ears can fulfill. If a tape recorder is used, it should be the scribe's duty to transcribe into writing everything before the next working so that it can be reviewed.

"To do magick without a record is like trying to run a business without book-keeping."[6] Throughout his books Crowley continually uses such examples as to why a diary is needed, adding, "if you call in an auditor to investigate a business, and when he asks for the books you tell him that you have not thought it worth while to keep any, you need not be surprised if he thinks you every kind of an ass."[7] With time, a knack will come about how to use your Magickal Record. This will become apparent in relationship to your rituals as you continually review what has transpired and build off the past, and you'll become driven by the revelations to pursue further communications.

One of my students once asked about the difficulties he was having setting up the exact same elemental qualities on the following evening that mimicked the original birth pangs of the elemental on the first night. He wanted to continue with the same communications. I reminded him that he must regulate his hours; a nightly venture is OK but make sure the time remains the same. The major requirement when working with an elemental through a Ouija board is the foundation you've set which allowed the elemental to be brought to birth in the first place, and if you summon an elemental on a given day and time, evoke only that elemental force and no other.

Some magicians have long argued that an elemental has no defined "image" in his particular elemental sphere, and that such is determined only by the qualities of the overall ruling attributes one was working when the elemental was *first* evoked. True, an elemental is a pure being without form or substance, yet by planning the type of door through which the elemental can communicate you have eliminated much of the guesswork to his nature. In many ways the elemental is just like you. He was brought to birth at one specific time, and as each day continues he is affected by the astrological qualities of the tides and forces that are bathing our Earth.

CHAPTER NINE

"There is, however, a good way of using this instrument to get what you want, and that is to perform the whole operation in a consecrated circle, so that undesirable aliens cannot interfere with it. You should then employ the proper magical invocation in order to get into your circle just the one spirit you want. It is comparatively easy to do this. A few simple instructions are all that is necessary, and I shall be pleased to give these, free of charge, to any one who cares to apply."

—ALEISTER CROWLEY

Only a fool would spend precious time and energy building a glorious Temple in the belief that it will automatically attract invisible beings; this achieves little except the praise of others who are in awe of the pretty room. Like attracts like on every plane. Case studies of poltergeists show that a Temple is not needed for them to be invited into your house. You should take this into consideration when beginning your Ouija workings. Those who have studied Enochian history will tell you that John Dee performed his angelic magick throughout Europe in regular rooms and halls simply by transferring the whole, or part thereof, into a sacred space. Creating a permanent space is not required, but regarding the establishment of a sacred space there is one thing we need to discuss: the proper use of one's imagination. This is the single most important tool that will enable you to set up your Temple and magick circle. Without such, a room is just a room.

It can be argued that use of the term "imagination" implies a falsity created by the mind to patronize a belief, but this lacks an appreciation of magickal application. After all, many religious moments begin when an individual lets his or her imagination flow deep within in regard to their prayers or faith. If done correctly, they come away with a sense of connecting with their God. What is the difference if a magician does it under a controlled circumstance? Although imagination is a tool of the subject's mind, we also know that if an individual allows his thoughts to drift far enough out into the astral waters something happens, and no mortal can tell the distinction. Imagination gives us the ability to clothe our deities and our surroundings in an appropriate astral vehicle whereby they and us unite, where it is almost impossible to tell the difference whether the imagery is coming *from* the mind or *through* it.

Lack of imagination is the major reason why some people can recite magickal incantations and achieve absolutely nothing while others open up hidden gateways. Most invisible entities are attracted by inward aspirations, not necessarily verbose ramblings. I must again emphasize that these entities have access to regions of your mind that you don't. For any ritual to be successful, you must be sure that what you're attempting is in perfect conformity with your True Will. Deep in a person's mind, they often lack the conviction that a ritual is really going to work. This lack of confidence can short-circuit the ritual long before it ever begins. In other words, if you don't fully believe in what you're doing, neither will the elemental. He, like most invisible beings, acts in relationship to your faith in yourself.

The elemental is always out to please his master, even if it's to prove its master's own deep unconscious disbelief in his own existence. This may seem like a double-edged sword and, in fact, it is. The grave danger is that just because you lack the belief that the entity is real doesn't mean that he doesn't exist. By playing in the astral waters you may accidentally open a permanent door into your house while believing nothing has happened. Many an elemental has tricked humans this way and gained access into our world; shortly thereafter the unsuspecting magician, or other members of his household, may begin to hear bumping, crashing noises and weird sliding sounds around his house.

You must clearly know the reason why you want to do an elemental working and what you wish to achieve. When you do a ritual and read the incantations, you use your "imagination" in a certain fashion that affects the astral plane. Although inward and outward aspirations go hand in hand, the inward concentration is what attracts the elemental. It's like an eternal flame burning in darkness to guide an entity toward the shores of our reality. On the other hand, Ouija workings always attract "something," considering the plethora of divergent beings just waiting on the other side to slip through the door. The real hazard lies in not attracting what you want while allowing just any old entity through that door. The whole purpose of this book is to teach control: Crowley wrote that once an entity has been drawn through a Ouija board, the "establishment of the identity of a spirit by ordinary methods is a very difficult problem."[1] The type of entity, not necessarily its name, must be determined long before it is allowed to manifest. Otherwise, it is usually impossible to determine if the invisible entity is good or malefic until it's too late.

Regarding the manifestation of an elemental, it has long been debated whether a Temple, robes, magickal implements and other forms of paraphernalia are all that important. This is something up to the individual; however, simplicity is the key. Some things are mandatory for control and protection. The strongest argument for most mundane ritualistic props is that they help an individual set his own mood, which in turn affects an elemental's behavior. Anything you think in regard to the implements and the ritual becomes real to the elemental.

On an archetypal level, without any human intervention, the laws inherent in certain symbols will always bind the elemental. This is because the laws of this plane on which the mundane implement resides, and the astral plane that contains its invisible opposite, bind a symbol such as the magickal chain. Everything has an opposite: one visible and the other invisible. A positive and a negative. The mere fact that something was created implies someone had to think about its use and thus they projected their thoughts onto the astral in regard to that item. If you've obtained a chain, but lack a strong conviction that the elemental will be bound by it, it won't.

Everything we've mentioned dealing with astral or archetypal symbols inherent in the elemental kingdom does not necessarily mean that any entity is completely bound by those Laws if you've given it an unconscious license to ignore it. The key is *without any human intervention*. Astrally it must follow its own Laws. However, when you obtained the chain for ritualistic purposes, you projected your ideas pertaining to that particular item onto the astral. If there is a weak or broken link in "your" chain, it is due to your personal convictions about its ability to do the job correctly. The same holds true for most religious objects used by priests and others who attempt exorcisms or similar dealings with denizens of the invisible kingdoms. Their faith and imagination must be unbending and strong—if they waver for even a split second they stand the chance of losing all. A member of the Hermetic Order of the Golden Dawn said it best when he wrote: "When a man imagines he actually creates a form on the Astral or even on some higher plane; and this form is as real and objective to intelligent beings on that plane, as our earthly surroundings are to us."[2] Faith does move mountains, and imagination should not be idly wasted.

Years ago, at the beginning of every board ritual I attended, we meditated to get into a relaxed state. This usually took about fifteen minutes. It was mandatory and important for the astral waters within each of us to become calm in preparation for our thoughts being cast into the astral correctly. Afterward whatever we thought became extremely vivid and real to the inhabitants of the astral. My teacher often warned us of a side effect caused by our playing in these astral waters: "Your thoughts cast into the astral waters are like rocks being thrown into a pond." The intensity with which we think and use our imagination implies the direction as well as how far we're able to throw the rock. And when the rock hits the waters, like our own thoughts, it creates ripples. The ripples are like someone shaking a spider's web, sending out subtle vibrations toward a waiting spider that feels the vibrations and is drawn toward the source. Remember this analogy, because those who unconsciously wander into a spider's lair often become its victims, as in the case of poltergeist activities. Someone, whether present now or a previous tenant, cast rocks where they shouldn't have and attracted an unwanted visitor. Where the rock is thrown and where it lands should be carefully planned. The lesson here is control: knowing exactly what we are summoning and what to do once it crawls upon the shores of our reality.

Beginners often overlook the ripple effect on the astral waters. This is often mistakenly equated to karma by those who claim it to be an astral retribution because an individual is tampering with things he shouldn't be doing. However, this often-equated "slap" is simply part of the cause and effect, and has nothing to do whether you're doing something right or wrong, but with an unprepared magician. When a rock, or thought, hits the astral waters, it sends out ripples in all directions, including back toward us. This is the origin of the karmic slap.

On a daily level most thoughts rarely create large enough ripples or waves with an intensity enough to do serious harm to our reality when they wash back up onto the shore. Everyone deals constantly with these ripples; it's part of life. We all think, and it is only natural that such thought affects how we function in the mundane world. However, on a magickal level, due to the intensity of our imagination which is likened to a large rock, the ripples can be equated to a tidal wave. If your tiny island, your inward self, is not 100% protected, it stands the chance of being devastated which naturally affects the conscious mind of the magician—thus, the slap. The only true protection is a properly prepared psyche which has been strengthened to accept the ripples, or the tidal wave. It's all the same thing no matter what terms you use to describe it: currents, Tattwas or tides, astral waters, tidal waves and ripples.

When you do a proper ritual, something courses through your system at an alarming rate. Exactly what that "something" is, is for you to label using the term with which you feel most comfortable—after all, they are just labels. Remember that a flimsy boat that ignores or tries to outrun a tidal wave by seeking sanctuary in a conscious reality will almost certainly be swamped, but a sturdy boat which holds its ground, knowing what is coming, goes headlong into the storm and often rides it out. *As Above, So Below.* The sturdy boat has the conviction of its faith. The bottom line is that you *wanted* to draw an entity to you, and threw a rock at him that splashed into the waters to get his attention; hopefully he'll surf the waves back toward your shore. Just be prepared for his arrival as well as the waves.

It is important that you read and re-read every single word you're planning to use when summoning an elemental. You must become extremely familiar with every word so that when you're speaking you can then focus your imagination on other things. In the very beginning when summoning the elemental, you should be imagining a door slowly opening in the direction from which he is coming. Then, far off in the distance, you should visualize the entity approaching. The stronger the visual image, the greater the chance of attracting the correct elemental. Since elementals are archetypal you should clothe them in the image of a brightly-lit colored ball. This is easiest to visualize for beginners. The best colors to use are yellow for air, red for fire, blue for water and a black or green ball of light for earth. With time, the image may solidify into something far more, but for starters a simpler image is better. You'll be able to focus your imagination as it approaches. If you desire to use a different symbol other than a colored ball, remember the golden rule that elementals are archetypal. Clothe them appropriately and by doing this no other entity can slip in.

When using Enochian magick some magicians place the correct Watchtower on the wall toward the direction in which they're summoning the elemental. While doing the actual evocation they imagine the entity as a tiny ball of spinning light, getting larger and larger as it slowly descends through the Watchtower. These Watchtowers are very complicated talismans or doorways and require much study to be fully appreciated, especially in relationship to a Temple.

Years ago, at the Brocken Mountain Lodge OTO in Connecticut, its Temple was draped in black cloth. This gave the room a unique atmosphere when lit by candlelight, especially when incense was heavily burned. The corners of the room virtually disappeared and everyone felt as if they were standing in the blackness of infinity. To understand this Temple we handed out an Enochian Paper titled *The Cube*, which explained to the novice that "Our floor is a cube, you cannot see its sides, or its bottom. You are standing upon its top. This cube is our Earth and square, not round is the shape. It is floating in the midst of the blackness called space."[3] The paper then elaborated that although the Watchtowers hung on our walls, there are no walls to an invisible being. The sacred gates of the universe are floating or suspended in the blackness of infinite space. "When an individual realizes that the Temple is actually a fortress which borders on the realm of the Abyss he begins to see the vast wilderness which lay just beyond the gate (Watchtower) and thus the importance of these gates is seen. For it is through these gates that the desired entity when evoked will enter into our universe and manifest in our Temple. These doorways are both sacred and dangerous."[4]

The ceremonial circle, which we'll discuss later in this chapter, will protect everyone within its boundaries and will act as a fortress on the edge of the Abyss of Choronzon, "wherein whosoever entereth he shall be at safety as within a fortified Castle, and nothing shall be able to harm you."[5] Although Choronzon is said to reside in the 10th Aethyr, his realm automatically extends to the outer walls of a magician's circle. Once drawn and consecrated this is the astral or archetypal quality of a circle. It acts as a Holy City where "the armies of Light are set against the outermost Abyss, against the horror of emptiness, and the malice of Choronzon."[6] This comment comes from Crowley's vision of the 11th Enochian Aethyr or realm called IKH,[7] which lies just before the realm of Choronzon. The entire vision should be carefully studied in Crowley's *The Vision & The Voice*. It will give a clearer understanding of the circle and its relationship to the realm of Shells, especially considering the workings of a Ouija board. All in all, the circle is a general part of the heritage of most magickal practices from ceremonial magicians to wiccan.

The Watchtowers, which act as doorways in the imaginary walls of this fortress, are guarded by the four great archangels, Michael, Gabriel, Raphael and Uriel, who can vanquish Choronzon by the mere presence of their Light. When any one of these gates is opened an elemental can enter into the circle, if only to move the triangle of the Ouija board. While doing the evocation it is vastly important to use your imagination to slowly bring the entity into the triangle. Once there, command his actions to be bound within its confines throughout the duration of the ritual or until such a time as he is given the License to Depart. However, in almost every case, the elemental is actually still on his own plane or just beyond the walls of the circle. When you imagine the ball slowly entering into the triangle it does not necessarily imply that the elemental is there himself as much as you've given him the ability to use the implement as a means of communication. I have witnessed one magician command the entity to "Lay his hands upon the triangle!" This imparts a much clearer image of the ball descending as if an entity was stretching forth its hand while standing outside the circle. Although rare, entities may enter the circle by means of the Watchtowers. This is why you must bind them within the triangle whether you feel that they are within the circle or not.

The bottom line is that all rituals should contain visualization. Without the use of our imagination we lack control. Some sort of visual imagery must accompany everything you do. If you use a Magickal Sword or a Dagger as an implement to control the elemental, you must imagine the elemental in a submissive role at your command while pointing said implement at him. If you're wondering how you can point a Dagger at an invisible entity, it's quite simple. An elemental will always be bound within a given area by your imagination, and that should be the triangle or planchette used with the Ouija board. It is toward this implement that you point the Dagger.

Invisible entities, especially lower elementals, have been known to use any ploy as a means to make you to think they're elsewhere so that you will break his tethers, but always remember, you bound the entity within the triangle and that is where he is. If it has broken loose it is because you let him out. Avoid using any phrases or terms that imply the entity's location is anywhere other than inside the triangle, and continually stress throughout your conversation that he is bound to remain in the triangle. This should be done for no other reason than to consciously reinforce it to yourself so that you don't slip up.

Lower elementals may try to escape, being tricksters of sorts, but they can only do such at your command, not theirs.

I must remind you: it is not an evil being as much as a three-year-old child who wants to play. Be verbally on guard at all times. For instance, if you consciously ask if the bumps, creaks and noises which you hear around your house are him and he answers yes, then you've acknowledged him free of the triangle and have allowed him to escape. On the other hand, it is OK to ask how he is creating the noises when confined within the triangle, and express this aspect strongly. He may try to trick you with answers such as "I am not bound within the triangle," but this is not true. Instead, command him to remain within the triangle and do it forcibly. Then change the subject and move the topic into another area of thought. His abilities do in fact allow him to create noises or reactions outside the triangle, both during a ritual and at other times, but these are all temporary manifestations. It's only logical that if an entity standing outside the circle is able to move the triangle, he is also capable of moving objects and creating noises around the house, especially in those areas not confined within the circle. However, he can do nothing within the circle where you are protected unless you allow him.

The circle defines your sacred space. In beginning a ritual working with a Ouija board, an imaginary circle should be drawn around the entire room. Visualize a burning wall of fire as you slowly point your finger or magickal Dagger toward the ground while walking in a circular fashion around the room. Everyone present must remain within the confines of this image throughout the ritual. Under no circumstance should anyone be allowed to leave. If they do, it will send a message that they have no faith in the strength of the image, and this will be projected onto the astral as a break in the circle. This simple mundane act could allow any stray entity to be unleashed into your house to mess with your communications and threaten the lives of all present.

We have already warned of the dangers of allowing just any entity to communicate, as did Aleister Crowley with his distaste of people who communicate with "any stray intelligence that may be wandering about" and of those who "use the Ouija Board without taking the slightest precautions."[8] You need to be in complete control of your astral surroundings during the ritual, defining a space in a circular fashion to depict the universe in which the working shall take place, and then "cleaning house" by banishing everything within the circle. This requirement will be explained in the next chapter. You must consider yourself a scientist who requires a clean workspace and germ-free environment so that the experiments will not be tainted or contaminated. Just as a scientist can use precautions when leaving his surroundings to safeguard against unwanted bacteria or viruses from escaping into our world, magicians are also taught ways of leaving a circle without astrally breaching the image. For now, follow the simple rule: no one leaves the circle, even in their own thoughts.

I was once asked if it was all right to imagine pure white light instead of fire when drawing a magickal circle. Although it might work by the mere nature of one's belief, it lacks the appropriate archetypal symbolism to bridge the above with the below needed in full ritual workings such as Enochian or Ouija magick. These formulas should be considered similar to mathematical equations which have been time-tested, and you should learn these principles before attempting to impress your own personal ideas and proclivities upon the astral. On an astral level anything you think or design becomes true, but there are dangers in thinking this is justifiable with every type of working. When a magickal ritual deals primarily with yourself in regard to personal initiation or basic rites of worship, you can utilize a more personal approach to structure. However, when you're working with real invisible entities you must learn the correct archetypal laws which govern their world rather than your own.

The circle which you have drawn in your room resides on the mundane plane, although it also has the capability of being temporarily outside it. This reflects its ability to be two circles at once: one in reality and the other on the astral. This particular quality of the circle is mandatory to grasp. The problem for most people is that after drawing a circle their reality appears to be the same and the invisible is, of course, still invisible, but the magician knows that he has created a sacred space which exists between the two worlds. That is the key.

Although this "between" state is often mentioned theoretically, it is rarely explained adequately. If something lies between, it is neither astral nor mundane, but what is it? This state is produced by the union of two circles. Together these two circles are symbolically male and female, or reality and astral. When united they will create a door whereby an entity, or child, is brought to birth. These two circles when correctly intersected create an ancient symbol known as the Vesica Piscis. This oval figure, pointed at top and bottom, is similar in theory to a magician's triangle, especially that of a Ouija board. How a circle works is far more intricate than most are aware.

The actual formation of a circle is easy. In many old grimoires the magician was told to take the Sickle, the implement of Choronzon, and stick it into the center of the place where the Circle was to be made. This defines the perimeter of Choronzon's world in relationship to our own universe, like drawing a line in the dirt. After the magician sticks the Sickle in the ground he is told to take a cord nine feet in length, fasten one end onto the Sickle, and with the other end trace out the circumference of the Circle, which he is to mark either with the sword or with the knife. This implement signifies the strength of the magician as well as the circle itself which he has just drawn. Unfortunately, sticking a sickle in your parlor rug or kitchen floor sometimes has a negative effect when later seen by those not directly partaking in the ritual, like the landlord. In this case, use your imagination to create the circle. You can also create a circle made of cloth to be rolled out and placed around the room when needed, or of smaller pieces of cut wood laid down upon the floor, piece after piece, until such becomes a full circle. The thoughts that go into making these circles help strengthen the astral image.

The portable circle is to be laid out before the ritual begins, and you should still go through the motions of visualizing a burning wall of fire as you slowly point your magickal dagger toward the circle's perimeter while walking, in a circular fashion, around the room. In all cases the circles I have seen were about six inches wide, some white with a green border inside and out. It is all right for you to design an actual circle which reflects your own ritual and beliefs. For instance, you can write upon the circle the appropriate names of the archangels or the four sacred names which you vibrated toward the four quarters. Not only will these names help to define the quarterly directions (East, South, West and North), but they also act as protection against unwanted guests.

After a circle has been drawn and banished, or cleansed, everything within the circle should be consecrated. This implies affirming its sacredness not only to yourself but to the Gods. There are many types of Consecration Rituals but there is an excellent example found in a book called *The Magus*. Here the magician makes his affirmation by saying:

"In the name of the holy, blessed, and glorious Trinity, proceed we to our work in these mysteries to accomplish that which we desire; we therefore, in the names aforesaid, consecrate this piece of ground for our defense, so that no spirit whatsoever shall be able to break these boundaries, neither be able to cause injury nor detriment to any of us here assembled; but that they may be compelled to stand before the circle, and answer truly our demands, so far as it pleaseth Him who liveth for ever and ever and who says, I am Alpha and Omega, the Beginning and the End, which is, and which was, and which is to come, the Almighty; I am the First and the Last, who am living and was dead; and behold I live forever

and ever; and I have the keys of death and hell. Bless O Lord! this creature of earth wherein we stand; confirm, O God! thy strength in us, so that neither the adversary nor any evil things may cause us to fail, through the merits of Jesus Christ. Amen."[9]

This is a very old aeonic Consecration Ritual. There are newer versions which Aleister Crowley recommends in his opus *Magick in Theory & Practice,* Chapter XIV, on Consecrations. In Crowley's version the magician simply raises his arms, thinks of his Holy Guardian Angel and consecrates everything within the circle by loudly proclaiming: "I am uplifted in thine heart; and the Kisses of the stars rain hard upon thy body." (Al II:62) While he proclaims this, the magician imagines everything within the circle being bathed in a bright white light with all evil or negativity being cast outside the circle. The above old aeonic version is to provide you with another idea in case you wish to design your own Consecration Ritual based on your beliefs.

Within the circle itself you should have absolutely no furniture or items unrelated to the ritual at hand. I have not mentioned many of the implements used in a magician's repertoire because most will not be immediately needed. Less is always more in a Ouija board ritual. Besides, there are many excellent volumes like Aleister Crowley's *Book 4* or *Magick in Theory & Practice* which explain the symbology and use of these implements. Some items you may wish to bring in at a later date when the need arises. Whatever you decide upon, be sure you understand its magickal and archetypal symbology completely. No items should be randomly used in a ritual simply because you "think" they should be there. Like a true scientist you should not be using things you do not fully understand.

At first, all you need is a table and chairs, which could be as simple as dragging the kitchen table or coffee table into the middle of a room so that a sizable "imaginary" circle can be drawn around it. Crowley says that although "the Magician has been limited in his choice of room, he is more or less able to choose what part of the room he will work in. He will consider convenience and possibility. His circle should not be too small and cramp his movement; it should not be so large that he have long distance to traverse. Once the circle is made and consecrated, the Magician must not leave it, or even lean outside, lest he be destroyed by the hostile forces that are without."[10] Be sure the circle is large enough to allow adequate movement to perform the ritual. If anyone in the room is in danger of accidentally falling, or reaching, beyond the circle, then the room is too small and you must reconsider your area.

Also, there should be absolutely *no electric lights* or electrical devices used during the ritual if at all possible. Only candles are to be permitted. It is generally believed that strong electrical currents affect most invisible entities, and I tend to agree from my own personal experience. Electrical current, equating elementally with fire, somehow disrupts the astral waters. My own teacher said that a good Ouija working should be held in a room where there is the least amount of electrical gadgetry present, including such things as wall outlets, lights and other obvious wires where electrical current is allowed to flow. Remember, even though a light is off, its cord may still be plugged into a wall outlet and there is still electricity flowing through the wires up to the on/off switch.

If the wires are within a wall then this is something that can't be avoided, but other electrical currents can be dealt with very easily. I would suggest unplugging all electrical appliances in the room where you're going to do your ritual. This will limit the current to being only within the walls and will avoid having the electricity snaking around the room through one cord and appliance after another. You should also note in your Magickal Diary the location of all known outlets. These can affect the ritual depending upon the direction in which they are situated and the elemental quality ruling that area in contrast to the elemental being evoked. If at all possible, always avoid rooms which have wall outlets in the direction from which you're summoning the elemental. Better yet, if it does not affect the house functions too badly, throw the circuit breaker to cut off all electricity in the area in which you're working. All in all, less electrical current means greater success.

I have also partaken in wiccan ceremonies where candles had been placed outside the circle on the mantel of the fireplace, corner tables, windowsills and other areas to illuminate the room. This is a very bad idea from a magickal point of view. Think carefully before you casually set up your sacred space. All the lighting needs for the ritual should be placed within the circle. There are only a few exceptions to this rule, where lamps are placed just outside the circle, but these have a different purpose than illumination. The number of these lamps may vary depending upon one's ritualistic needs but usually nine lamps or candles are placed on small pentagrams on the floor just outside the perimeter of the circle. All candles must be close enough to the circle in case there is a fire problem and if they need to be extinguished by a hearty puff of air. Under no circumstance is a magician to reach beyond the circle with their hands unless he or she is aware of the dire consequences of their actions. If the candle is too far and a problem arises, then a mundane breach of the circle is mandatory to alleviate the problem, and it also means the entity can escape because of your actions.

Crowley explains further the purpose of the lamps: "Without the Circle are nine pentagrams equidistant, in the centre of each of which burns a small Lamp; these are the 'Fortresses upon the Frontiers of the Abyss.' They keep off those forces of darkness which might otherwise break in." He continues by explaining, "These nine lamps were originally candles made of human fat, the fat of enemies slain by the Magician; they serve as warnings to any hostile force of what might be expected if it cause trouble. To-day such candles are difficult to procure; and it is perhaps simplest to use beeswax."[11]

He is right; candles of human fat cannot be easily procured at your local store. Regular candles will be sufficient as long as they are "virgin"—new and never used for any other purpose. It is always a good idea to test an extra candle long before a ritual to carefully time how long it will take for it to burn down. You don't want part of the defense which keeps off "those forces of darkness which might otherwise break in" slowly burning out during the ritual. In fact, it is highly recommended that oil lamps be used outside the circle and not candles.

Some will say that you must purify each and every item within the circle, but in Ouija workings this is not completely necessary. Purification simply implies oneness to a purpose. This is expressed first by yourself and then by everyone else who is present. It means that all the implements and paraphernalia within the circle are there for only one reason and that is for the ritual. Crowley uses an excellent analogy with electricity: "If insulation is imperfect, the whole current goes back to earth. It is useless to plead that in all those miles of wire there is only one-hundredth of an inch unprotected."[12] Everything within the circle must have a direct purpose in the ritual itself with no excuses. Any random items brought into the circle can act like a frayed wire. Crowley states that "The first task of the Magician in every ceremony is therefore to render his Circle absolutely impregnable."[13] Never forget this.

Magicians also ring a bell before the actual ritual begins, usually after the nine candles have been lit and the circle has been drawn. This is done to call the Universe to attention. The sacred bell is often attached to the chain of 333 links, which we previously mentioned as relating to Choronzon. Crowley writes, "At the sound of this Bell the Universe ceases for an indivisible moment of time, and attends to the Will of the Magician."[14] Afterward the "Intent" or a Magickal Oath is read. This Oath is nothing more than a statement, carefully written beforehand, which will remind everyone in the ritual chamber, both visible and invisible, what you're attempting to achieve. It should be scrutinized for loopholes. Remember the story of the magician doing an elaborate ritual in quest of money only to discover a penny on the sidewalk—some might think he magickally failed to achieve his goal, but did he? There is absolutely no way to explain what you should be writing in your intent since no two rituals are ever alike. This is something that only becomes apparent through careful contemplation plus trial and error. Do not take this aspect of the ritual lightly; your entire success depends upon it. I might add that a shorter intent is far better than one which is long and rambling, so be concise and to the point.

In the actual evocation, it is best for the beginner to simply use the Earth of Earth Enochian call. This will be given in the next chapter. Always remember what Aleister Crowley wrote about evocations; "The whole secret may be summarised in these four words: 'Enflame thyself in praying'."[15]

Once the planchette begins to move, you can ask the questions for which you seek answers. At the end of the evening you will want to give the entity a License to Depart rather than immediately banishing him. This implies more than the courtesy of simply saying "Good-bye" in Ouija board jargon. In fact, the License to Depart follows directly after the entity has moved the triangle toward the section of the board where the word Good-bye is written. You'll also want to do this License mainly because of residue: although the entity has been dismissed, or left, there is always something which remains, or even something which might be attracted to the circle by the vacuum created by the elemental in its leaving. The License guarantees that whoever had hoped to slip into our world will be dismissed. It is virtually impossible to have an operation that runs smoothly without leaving such residue; Crowley acknowledges this, warning us that this type of residue "must be duly dispersed, or they will degenerate and become evil."[16]

The greatest evil is the obsession or possession of an individual's psychic system to which the residue attaches itself after the ritual. This could occur within hours or weeks or longer; there is no set rule of thumb. So it is important to always use a License to Depart even if nothing appears and the triangle hasn't moved. If an entity has remained quiet, being a trickster of sorts, you must forcibly let him know that he must depart forthwith or soon he'll be banished into the oblivion of Choronzon's realm of Shells. Few elementals will risk such a fate.

Some of the old magickal grimoires have excellent examples of the License to Depart, or The Discharge as some call it. Most of these are simply thanking the spirit or elemental for diligently answering unto your demands and questions. Further explain that you give him the license to depart from the premise in peace and quiet, but request that he be ready to come again when beckoned. The discharge is usually a very brief but courteous good-bye to all the forces. A classic example of a License to Depart is found in the ancient *Grimoire of Armadel*. Here the magician simply recites to the spirit:

"Seeing that peaceably and in quiet thou hast come, and has made answer unto me in this my petition, I return thanks unto God, in Whose Name thou hast come. Depart hence unto thine habitations, and be thou ready to return whensoever I shall have called thee. Through Christ our Lord! Amen."[17]

I personally like the flow of this license and have used such in the past, omitting the reference to Christ. It is also permissible for you to design your own license as long as the wording is something you strongly believe in. Crowley gives an excellent example of the License: a magician should briefly say, "And now I say unto thee, depart in peace unto thine habitations and abodes—and may the blessings of the Highest be upon thee in the names of (here mention the divine name suitable to the operation, or a Name appropriate to redeem that spirit); and let there be peace between thee and me and be thou very ready to come, whensoever thou art invoked and called!"[18]

Regarding the Magickal Diary in relationship to the License to Depart, Crowley writes: "Immediately after the License to Depart, and the general closing up of the work, it is necessary that the Magician should sit down and write up his magickal record. However much he may have been tired by the ceremony, he ought to force himself to do this until it become habit. Verily, it is better to fail in the magical ceremony than to fail in writing down an accurate record of it."[19]

It might be difficult to grasp exactly what you are supposed to do point by point when ritualistically using a Ouija board; these chapters are meant more for theory rather than step-by-step lessons. At the end of the book I have put together a suggested ritual that you may or may not wish to use, but hopefully it will give you ideas in relationship to what you have read. If you're serious, you must fine-tune these steps to suit yourself. No two people's needs are alike. However, there are many good magickal volumes that can aid you in your study, and most will at least give you the preliminaries. The more you read, the more ritualistic requirements you may want to bring into your Ouija board working.

Yet this particular method of communication has worked very successfully without any ritualistic formalities for hundreds of years, and arguably most of what I have been discussing is not needed to make the board work. The basic requirements, precautions and theories expressed in this book are designed to allow you to achieve far better control over whom you decide to bring through the board. How elaborate you wish to go with the ritual is up to you; this usually depends on the type of entity with whom you desire to communicate. As a rule of thumb the Enochian Angels require much, as do other spiritual hierarchies. With elementals and earth-bound entities, the ritual can be so simple that merely the laying of hands upon a planchette can summon them forth. Never forget that you're a scientist. Start small and with each new experiment try something different. If you're successful, then add it to the already proven magickal repertoire that you're establishing. It is far better to slowly elaborate the ritual than to begin with something verbose and boring.

You will quickly learn that the astral plane is a very odd place to play. In the beginning, when you are preparing your Temple space and trying to obtain your magickal implements, strange things begin to occur. Crowley says it best: "Just as soon as you start seriously to prepare a place for magical work, the world goes more cockeyed than it is already. Don't be surprised if you find that six weeks' intense shopping ... fails to provide you with some simple requisite that normally you could buy in ten minutes. Perhaps your fires simply refuse to burn, even when liberally dosed with petrol and phosphorus, with a handful of Chlorate of Potash thrown in just to show that there is no ill feeling! When you have almost decided that you had better make up your mind to do without something that seems really quite unobtainable—say, a sixty-carat diamond which would look so well on the head-dress—a perfect stranger comes along and makes you a present of one. Or, a long series of quite unreasonable obstacles or silly accidents interfere with your plans: or, the worst difficulties in your way is incomprehensibly removed by some extraordinary 'freak of chance.' Or ... In a word, you seem to have strolled into a world where—well, it might be going too far to say that the Law of Cause and Effect is suspended; but at least the Law of Probability seems to be playing practical jokes on you. This means that your maneuvers have somehow attracted the notice of the Astral Plane: your new neighbors are taking an interest in the latest Tenderfoot, some to welcome, to do all they can to help you to settle down, others indignant or apprehensive at this disturbance of routine."[20] Yes, pilgrim, there is much a tenderfoot has to learn.

CHAPTER TEN

"Success is thy proof: argue not; convert not; talk not overmuch"
—*LIBER AL VEL LEGIS* III:42

I s it contradictory that I have written an entire book about the proper use of a Ouija board, when Aleister Crowley said "A few simple instructions are all that is necessary"? I agree with the Beast, but also felt that a volume was needed to reflect upon the history, the theories behind the board's movement and its relationship to new aeonic magick. Here I will state what is required, point by point.

The sample ritual in this chapter is solely to be used for evocation of an Enochian Earth of Earth elemental. If you have success with this elemental, and you wish to continue in your pursuit of exploring the astral plane, I would highly suggest picking up a good book on Enochian Magick which can teach you the next Calls and names required.

As noted, inevitably you'll need to evoke four separate elementals before you have mastered and controlled the Earth element itself.

In the ritual below you will notice that in order to invoke an elemental of <u>Earth of Earth</u> you will be using the 5th Enochian Call and the god name CABALPT. To invoke the next elemental of Water of Earth you'll use the same ritual, but instead of the 5th Enochian Call you'll use the 14th, and the god name

CABALPT will be changed to ANAEEM. To invoke an elemental of Fire of Earth you'll use the 15th Enochian Call and the god name OSPMNIR. Finally, to invoke an elemental of Air of Earth you use the 13th Enochian Call and the god name ANGPOI.

Here are some ritual notes that you can use:

1. You must determine which room you're going to use and the size of the circle. You then place all the required furniture and paraphernalia within its perimeter. This will include a table and chairs for the Ouija board and its participants as well as other chairs for the scribe and/or guests. Everyone should take their place and get comfortable for a long haul if necessary. The magician should remain standing. There should be a table for a ceremonial dagger and a book of evocations and instructions written in full, point by point, so the magician can read from it easily if his memory needs to be refreshed. It is advisable in addition to the scribe that the magician should also have a pencil or pen on his table to jot down notes while asking questions. Extra loose paper is always a good idea. In fact, all participants, except the two working the board, should be taking notes regarding their feelings, impressions and observations which will be turned over to the scribe at the end of the ritual; he will enter these into the magickal record. A clock should be easily visible so that all present can see it clearly. Individuals must be able to jot down the time as often as the need arises. Remember, this is not a spectator sport, and all present must contribute something even if it's only notes and personal views.

2. Once everyone is comfortable, the magician uses his dagger to draw an astral circle around the room, beginning in the east and moving toward the south. He imagines it as a burning wall of flames.

3. After the circle is completed, everything within it needs to be consecrated. The magician does this by raising his hands upward and loudly proclaiming:

"I am uplifted in thine heart; and the Kisses of the stars rain hard upon thy body."

While the magician is proclaiming this statement he imagines everything within the circle being bathed in a bright white light. You should not blindly imagine this light flooding everywhere, or you'll destroy the circle that you've just established. While consecrating you must keep in your mind the circle's perimeter and simply picture all negativity and evil being blasted to the outskirts of the circle, or thrown just beyond it as the Light grows brighter and brighter within the circle. Once this is fulfilled the magician puts the dagger back upon the altar.

4. The magician then faces East, picks up the Bell and rings it three times, pauses, followed by five more rings, a pause, and finally three last rings. This totals 11. The Bell is then returned to the table/altar. Then, with arms outstretched, a magician should proclaim loudly:

"Do what thou wilt shall be the whole of the Law."

This signifies that the Ritual has begun. At this point everyone should try to relax, breathe deeply and quietly meditate on the Intent for a few minutes, or as long as it takes, to enflame thyself in prayer.

5. The magician then turns and faces North. He recites the 5th Enochian Key. Pronunciation may appear to be almost impossible after reviewing the Key, but Enochian is very guttural, almost animalistic in its vibratory aspects by bellowing

forth individual letters, or groups thereof, rather than the words as a whole. Most descriptions of how to pronounce the language contradict each other; all are seemingly authorities. In volume four of Regardie's *The Golden Dawn* is an excellent description for beginners which I'd suggest reading. Others might disagree, but the bottom line is to try; don't get hung up in the arguments about the correct way to pronounce the angelic tongue. Let your own angel guide you from within as you speak his language, and to hell with mortal clamoring. Also, do not rehearse these Calls. If you must, randomly choose different words to work upon. These Calls can be very, very dangerous and should never be uttered in their entirety outside of a ritual setting. No matter where you are, to utter these Calls opens the elemental gateways and allows invisible entities to descend into your world. As Grady McMurtry used to warn, there is no such thing as "just rehearsing."

The Fifth Key (Enochian)

Sapahe zodimii du-i-be, od noasa ta qu-a-nis, adarocahe dorepehal caosagi od faonutas peripeso ta-be-liore. Casareme A-me-ipezodi na-zodaretahe afa; od dalugare zodizodope zodelida caosaji tol-toregi; od zod-cahisa esiasacahe El ta-vi-vau; od iao-d tahilada das hubare pe-o-al; soba coremefa cahisa ta Ela Vaulasa od Quo-Co-Casabe. Eca niisa od darebesa quo-a-asa: fetahe-ar-ezodi od beliora: ia-ial eda-nasa cicalesa; bagile Ge-iad I-el!

Although it is not necessary to recite such, the English translation of this Call or Key is as follows:

The Mighty Sounds Have Entered The Third Angle And Are Become As Olives In The Olive Mount: Looking With Gladness On The Earth, And Dwelling In The Brightness Of The Heavens As Continual Comforters. Unto Whom I Fastened Pillars Of

Gladness 19 And Gave Them Vessels To Water The Earth With All Her Creatures. And They Are The Brothers Of The First And The Second, And The Beginning Of Their Own Seats, Which Are Garnished With Continual Burning Lamps 69636 Whose Numbers Are As The First, The Ends, And The Contents Of Time! Therefore Come Ye, And Obey Your Creation! Visit Us In Peace And Comfort! Conclude Us As Receivers Of Your Mysteries. Why? Our Lord Is All One!

6. Let the magician then recite:

"I, (repeat your name), a faithful servant of the omnipotent God, amicably, earnestly, and confidently demand and beseech you to appear placidly, affably, and favourably before me, immediately and without delay, and henceforth at any time I wish, through all the remaining journey of my life, I beseech you to grant all my petitions, and especially grant me Knowledge and Judgment in all things assigned to your Office and Ministry and that are accomplished by you, one and many. I command you to appear within the triangle [point to the traveller with dagger], to perform, and to complete, goodly, plainly, intelligibly, and perfectly, according to your Virtue, Power and Office, and according to the capacity of your Ministry, entrusted and committed to you by the omnipotent God. In the sacred name CABALPT, spirits of Earth, borne of Earth, thee I summon, Adore your Creator! — NANTA"

Once the magician has finished vibrating the last word NANTA, the two individuals place their fingers upon the triangle and *not before*. The magician then turns and stands. Facing the Ouija board he asks:

"Who has answered our summons?"

(THIS BEGINS THE DIALOGUE AND QUESTIONS WITH THE OUIJA BOARD)

One of the final things you should do is to ask the entity what is required next to enable him to communicate further, or if he'd like you communicate with him. You should also ask about any spiritual requirements for yourself and others who are doing the ritual. It is important to become a good vehicle which will enable you to more clearly understand the entity's messages. This balance of requirements, you moving inward and they outward, must be sought with every stage of a ritual, day after day. If an entity tells you that you need to do nothing yourself, then it is very important to *question its intent*. Why won't it help you? Most mortals are in need of spiritual help in unfolding their True Will, or Star. Do not be so pretentious in thinking otherwise or to allow your ego to be inflated because an entity says you're perfect. If an entity is not willing to give or offer advice in your spiritual quest, there is a reason, and the road one is walking is very dangerous and often one-sided. However, if the entities tell you to do certain things, then before the next ritual you must fulfill these obligations. Remember, no requirement should ever be to hurt another living being, human or animal.

Be sure to thank the elemental graciously for all his help and for the guidance that he has given during the night.

7. When the ritual is over, after the entity has said "Good-bye," the magician gives the License to Depart. Here is the License to be used for all four Earth Elementals:

"And now I say unto thee, depart in peace unto thine habitations and abodes—and may the blessings of the Highest be upon thee in the names of MOR DIAL HCTGA and in the name ICZHHCAL, the Great King of the North, Spirits of Earth let there be peace between thee and me, and be thou very ready to come, whensoever thou art invoked and called again!"

Knock once with the dagger.

8. The magician then banishes the entire room by loudly proclaiming:

"For pure will, unassuaged of purpose, delivered from the lust of result, is every way perfect."

Let the magician imagine the room being bathed in a bright white light as he states the above.

After performing the above banishing, if you still feel that something is not right, as if lingering negativity has been captured and confined within the house, you'll need to perform a full *Lesser Ritual of the Pentagram*. In most cases this is not needed.

I have given this ritual below, however; I have not given any instructions on its meaning, the symbology or how to perform it. Instead I have included a private magickal lesson on this subject that is given out by one of Aleister Crowley's A∴A∴ branches as an Appendix to this book. It will explain this ritual in depth.

A Banishing Ritual is something you'll want to commit to memory. Not only can it be used to banish lingering negativity at the end of a ritual, but also if something goes drastically wrong during the ritual, it can be used to cast out unwanted entities from your surroundings almost immediately. Again, I must point out, commit this ritual to memory. If problems have occurred due to your magickal working, you do not want to look for a book where the ritual is mentioned and try to learn it at that stage.

In the ritual below, it states that you should "make a pentagram with the proper weapon." First of all, the pentagram should always be drawn upright and not inverted. Since we are working with Earth elementals you should begin drawing the pentagram from the bottom left point upward toward the top, then downward toward the bottom right, etc.

The Lesser Ritual of the Pentagram

(i.) Touching the forehead, say *Ateh* (Unto Thee).

(ii.) Touching the breast, say *Malkuth* (The Kingdom).

(iii.) Touching the right shoulder, say *ve-Geburah* (and the Power).

(iv.) Touching the left shoulder, say *ve-Gedulah* (and the Glory).

(v.) Clasping the hands upon the breast, say *le-Olahm, Amen* (to the Ages, Amen).

(vi.) Turning to the East, make a pentagram with the proper weapon. Say *Yod He Vau He.*

(vii.) Turning to the South, the same, but say *Adonai.*

(viii.) Turning to the West, the same, but say *Ahih.*

(ix.) Turning to the North, the same, but say *Agla.*

(x.) Extending the arms in the form of a cross, say—

(xi.) *Before me Raphael,*

(xii.) *Behind me Gabriel,*

(xiii.) *On my right hand Michael,*

(xiv.) *On my left hand Auriel,*

(xv.) *for about me flames the Pentagram,*

(xvi.) *and in the Column stands the six-rayed Star.*

(xvii.–xxi.) Repeat (i.) to (v.), the "Qabalistic Cross."

9. The last thing, which the magician does, is to make an affirmation to all the participants that the ritual is over and that they are now permitted to leave the circle and move about freely. He does such by stating loudly:

"Love is the law, love under will."

The congregation should all clap as an acknowledgment that they understand the ritual is over, similar to ringing the Bell to announce the beginning. The nine candles are then extinguished. Be sure to pick up and store all the magickal implements and props immediately so as not to profane them by idle touch. This especially includes wrapping the Ouija board in white cloth and treating it from this day forward as sacred. It is now a consecrated implement.

10. The ritual just mentioned is purely optional. Crowley wrote that, in regard to the Ouija board, there is "a good way of using this instrument to get what you want, and that is to perform the whole operation in a consecrated circle, so that undesirable aliens cannot interfere with it. You should then employ the proper magical invocation in order to get into your circle just the one spirit you want. It is comparatively easy to do this." There are only two mandatory requirements a magician really needs to fulfill. First, you need to learn how to lay out a magickal circle and consecrate it. Second, figure out whom you want to contact through a Ouija board, research this entity and then use the appropriate invocations to summon it. Enochian is the easiest method to control elementals that have easy access into the realm of Shells.

11. The final stage of any ritual is the Magickal Record. Some people believe you should set aside at least an hour after every ritual to have an open discussion amongst those who attended, with the Scribe taking notes. If you decide to do this, anything said during these talks should be appended to the Scribe's Magickal Records and should at no time alter what was written during the ritual itself. Before you begin the next Ouija working, your Magickal Record should be carefully studied to reflect what has been achieved, what you still wish to know and the direction in which you desire to go. The greatest results, if not profound thoughts, are usually achieved through rituals that are done over a lengthy period of time while continually communicating with the same entity or into the same area of the astral.

AFTERWORD

I hope I've given you enough food for thought in regard to working the Ouija board as a magickal implement. It is not just coincidence that the board appeared toward the end of the last century at the beginning of the New Aeon of Aquarius. It may reflect an unconscious, evolutionary process of a magickal implement emerging for the spiritual growth of humanity, like Enochian Magick itself.

While not everyone will have found Truth in the pages of this book, or follow its words to the letter, a profound statement regarding magick comes to mind: "All words are false except deep in the mind of the writer ... or with those who are kindred spirits. Folly comes only to those who demand that their words are Truth for all to follow."[1] This book is an expression of my personal beliefs and studies spanning the years since I played with my first Ouija board back in 1966, yet magickally I know it can only be true in the light of the laws that encompass my own internal Star, the center of my Universe.

Remember the magickal axiom *As Above, So Below*. Just as the Universe has its own set of laws wherein our Sun is its center, so does each and every one of us. Each individual must experiment magickally, even with a Ouija board if need be, to determine what are the correct laws (i.e., beliefs) of their own Universe. No two stars are alike nor have they the same set of laws. If some of the things I have written can guide you in your quest then I am pleased; if you disagree with what I've written, that's OK too.Crowley's magickal system is very important to openly discuss. I've been lecturing on magick for some twenty-seven odd years within OTO Lodges, Chapters and other bodies to both initiates and visitors, and feel it is time to extend the information to a wider audience. To quote from *The*

Book of the Law, "Success is thy proof: argue not; convert not; talk not overmuch" (AL III:42) This book expresses my own success in what I have learned over the years, and, I hope, will inspire people to use the board correctly. I can only give forth my words to other pathfinders who'll dare to venture where I have ventured.

God is not dead. He exists along with his hosts, both good and evil. If you're prompted to run out and purchase a Ouija board to discover this Truth for yourself, I again remind you to read very carefully the back of the box.

"Ouija ... is only a game ... isn't it?"

ENDNOTES

CHAPTER ONE

1. Hunt, Stoker, *Ouija, The Most Dangerous Game* (New York: Harper & Row, 1976), p. 77.

2. Brittle, Gerald, *The Demonologist: The Extraordinary Career of Ed and Lorraine Warren* (New York: St. Martin's Paperbacks, 1991).

3. Crowley, Aleister, *The Goetia, The Lesser Key of Solomon the King* (Maine: Samuel Weiser, Inc., 1995), p. 18.

4. Brittle, p. 108.

5. Blatty, William Peter, *The Exorcist* (New York: Harper & Row, 1971).

6. Brittle, p. 109.

7. Erdmenn, Steve, "The Truth Behind The Exorcist," *Fate Magazine*, Vol. 28 No. 1, Issue 298 (January 1975), p. 50.

8. Hansen-Steiger, Sherry, and Brad Steiger, *Hollywood and the Supernatural* (New York: Berkeley Books, 1992), p. 168.

9. "Exorcist, Breaking Records, Spurs Nation Craze," *The New Haven Register*, Sunday, February 10, 1974.

10. Blatty, pp. 36–37.

11. "Bit of the Old Boy in Exorcism, But Ramsey Pooh-Poohs it Mostly," *New York Daily News*, Thursday, January 31, 1974.

CHAPTER TWO

1. Gruss, Edmond, and John Hotchkiss, *The Ouija Board: Doorway to the Occult* (Chicago: Moody Press, 1975) p. 28. Original quote from *The Literary Digest*, July 3, 1920, p. 66.

2. "William Fuld Made $1,000,000 On Ouija But Has No Faith In It," *The Baltimore Sun*, July 4, 1920.

3. *Ibid.*

4. *Ibid.*

5. "Claimant to Title of Ouija Board Craze Dies," *The Baltimore Sun*, November 19, 1939.

6. *Ibid.*

7. "Wm. Fuld is Killed in Fall from Roof, Support gives way while he is helping erect flagpole atop factory," *The Baltimore Sun*, February 25, 1927.

8. "Monopoly on Ouija," *The New York Times,* February 24, 1966.

9. Cuoco, E.M., Consumer Relations Administrator, Parker Brothers, letter to author dated January 27, 1997.

10. Ouija Board, Mystifying Oracle (Parker Brothers, 1992).

11. "Nothing Occult in Ouija, Federal Court Rules. Boards are Taxable, according to Opinion Handed Down by Judge Ros," *The Baltimore Sun*, June 2, 1921.

12. "Ouija Board is Taxable, Appellate Court Says. Judge Woods, in Richmond, Hands Down Opinion Affirming Baltimore Judgement," *The Baltimore Sun*, February 10, 1922.

13. *Ibid.*

14. "The Supreme Court Refuses to Say What It Thinks of Ouija," *The Baltimore Sun*, June 6, 1922.

CHAPTER THREE

1. Regardie, Israel, *The Tree of Life: A Study in Magic* (New York: Samuel Weiser, Inc., 1969), pp. 203–204.

2. Crowley, *The Goetia,* pp. 71–72.

3. Frater Achad, *Crystal Vision through Crystal Gazing* (Chicago: Yogi Publication Society, 1923), p. 39.

4. Crowley, Aleister, "The Ouija Board—A Note," *The International,* Vol. XI No. 10, October 1917 (New York), p. 319.

5. Brittle, p. 109.

6–7. Crowley, "The Ouija Board—A Note," p. 319.

8. Crowley, Aleister, *The Book of Thoth* (New York: Samuel Weiser Inc., 1973), p. 88.

9. Crowley, Aleister, book review: *Jap Heron: A Novel Written From The Ouija Board. The International*, Vol. XI No. 9, 1917 (New York), p. 284.

10. Tanner, Jerald and Sandra, *Joseph Smith & Money Digging* (Salt Lake City: Utah Lighthouse Ministry, 1970), p. 15.

11. Walters, Wesley P., *Joseph Smith's Bainbridge, NY Court Trials* (Salt Lake City: Utah Lighthouse Ministry, 1974), p. 127. For further study on the subject of "The Faculty of Abra" and its relationship to Mormonism I'd suggest Jerald and Sandra Tanner's book *Mormonism, Magic and Masonry* (Salt Lake City: Utah Lighthouse Ministry, 1988).

12. Mackey, Albert G., *A Lexicon of Freemasonry* (Pennsylvania: Moss, Brother & Company, 1859), p. 13.

13. Smith, Mrs. Hester Travers, *Voices from the Void: Six Years'*

Experience in Automatic Communications (London: William Rider and Sons, Ltd., 1919), pp. 102–103.

14. *Ibid.*, p. 106.

15. Cayce, Hugh Lynn, *Venture Inward* (New York: Harper & Row, 1964).

16–17. Crowley, Aleister, *Magick in Theory & Practice* (New York: Castle Books, 1965), p. 15.

18. Smith, *Voices*, p. 4.

19. *Ibid.*, p. 5.

20. *Ibid.*, p. 7.

21. *Ibid.*, pp. 72–73.

22. *Ibid.*, p. 92.

23. Hunt, p. 69.

24. Smith, *Voices,* p. 108.

25. Crowley, "The Ouija Board—A Note," p. 319.

CHAPTER FOUR

1. Crowley, Aleister, *Magick Without Tears* (Minnesota: Llewellyn Publications, 1973), p. 178.

2. Crowley, "The Ouija Board—A Note," p. 319.

3–5. Crowley, *Magick Without Tears*, p. 179.

6. *Ibid.*, p. 182.

CHAPTER FIVE

1. Laycock, Donald C., *The Complete Enochian Dictionary*, preface by Stephen Skinner (London: Askin Publishers, 1978), pp. 10–11.

2. *The Private Diary of Dr. John Dee*, ed. James Orchard Helliwell (London: The Camden Society, 1842), p. 11.

3. Dee, *Private Diary*, p. 11.

4. *Ibid.*, p. 13.

5. *Ibid.*, p. 14.

6. French, Peter J., *John Dee, The World of an Elizabethan Magus* (London: Routledge & Kegan Paul, 1972), p. 116.

7. Dee, John, *A True & Faithful Relation of John Dee*, ed. Meric Causabon (London: Askin Publishers, 1974), p. 91.

8. Crowley, Aleister, *The Vision & The Voice* (Texas: Sangreal Foundation, Inc., 1972), p. 7.

9. *Ibid.*, p. 196.

CHAPTER SIX

1. Dee, John, *A True & Faithful Relation of John Dee*, ed. Meric Causabon (London: Askin Publishers, 1974), p. 168.
2. *Ibid.*, p. 171.
3. *Ibid.*, p. 170.
4. *Ibid.*, p. 172.

CHAPTER SEVEN

1. Crowley, Aleister, *Magick Without Tears* (Minnesota: Llewellyn Publications, 1973), p. 182–83.
2. Hansen-Steiger, Sherry, and Brad Steiger, *Hollywood and the Supernatural* (New York: Berkley Books, 1992), p. 168.
3. Crowley, Aleister, *Book 4* (Texas: Sangreal Foundation, Inc., 1972), p. 66.
4–5. Crowley, Aleister, *The Qabalah of Aleister Crowley* (New York: Samuel Weiser, Inc., 1973), p. 32.
6. Crowley, Aleister, *Liber Aleph, The Book of Wisdom or Folly* (California: Thelema Publishing Company, 1962), p. 15.
7. Smith, Mrs. Hester Travers, *Voices from the Void: Six Years' Experience in Automatic Communications* (London: William Rider and Sons, Ltd., 1919), p. 71.
8. *Ibid.*, p. 108.
9. Crowley, Aleister, "Liber O vel Manus et Sagittae," *The Equinox*, Vol. I No. II (New York: Samuel Weiser, Inc., 1978), p. 13.

CHAPTER EIGHT

1. *The Secret Rituals of the O.T.O.*, edited by F. King (New York: Samuel Weiser, Inc. 1973) p.199.
2. Crowley, Aleister, *Magick Without Tears* (Minnesota: Llewellyn Publications, 1973), p. 286.
3. Crowley, Aleister, *Book 4* (Texas: Sangreal Foundation Inc., 1972), p. 71.
4. Smith, Mrs. Hester Travers, *Voices from the Void: Six Years' Experience in Automatic Communications* (London: William Rider and Sons, Ltd., 1919), p. 7.
5. *Ibid.*, p. 71.
6. Crowley, Aleister, *Magick in Theory & Practice* (New York: Castle Books, 1965), p. 141.
7. *Ibid.*

CHAPTER NINE

1. Crowley, "The Ouija Board—A Note," p. 319.

2. Frater Resurgam (Dr. Berridge), "Some Thought on the Imagination," *Astral Projection, Magic and Alchemy,* ed. Francis King (New York: Samuel Weiser Inc., 1975), p. 33.

3. Frater Achad Osher, *Liber XXI The Cube, A basic symbolic representation of the Enochian Temple in relationship to the Universe* (Connecticut: Brocken Mountain Lodge OTO, 1977), p. 2.

4. *Ibid.,* p. 4.

5. *The Greater Key of Solomon*, trans. S. Liddell MacGregor Mathers (Illinois: The de Laurence Company, 1914), p. 104.

6. Crowley, *The Vision & The Voice*, p. 152.

7. *Ibid.,* p. 21.

8. Crowley, "The Ouija Board—A Note," p. 319.

9. Barrett, Francis, "Of the Particular Composition of the Magic Circle being Book II Part III," *The Magus* (New York: University Books, Inc., 1967), p. 106.

10. *Ibid.,* p. 57.

11. *Ibid.,* p. 58.

12–13. Crowley, *Magick in Theory & Practice*, p. 101.

14. Crowley, *Book 4*, p. 112.

15. Crowley, *Magick in Theory & Practice*, p. 129.

16. *The Grimoire of Armadel*, trans. and ed. S.L. MacGregor Mathers (New York: Samuel Weiser Inc., 1980), p. 18.

17–18. Crowley, *Magick in Theory & Practice*, p. 139.

19. *Ibid.,* p. 140.

20. Crowley, *Magick Without Tears*, p. 171.

CHAPTER TEN

1. "Editorial," *Hell-Spawn, The Magickal Writings of Brocken Spectres*, No. 1 (Connecticut: Brocken Mountain Lodge, OTO, An. LXXIX e.n., March 1984), p. 1.

2. Crowley, Aleister, *The Heart of the Master* (Canada: 93 Publishing, 1973), p. 9.

APPENDIX

The Magickal Essence of Aleister Crowley is a series of lessons which are privately distributed in one of Crowley's A∴A∴ branches. We thank this branch for the kind permission to quote it in full in this Appendix.

THE MAGICKAL ESSENCE OF CROWLEY

Understanding the New Aeon through the teachings of the Great Beast.

Epistle No. 13

~ An Open Letter
on the Lesser Ritual
of the Pentagram ~

Do what thou wilt shall be the whole of the law.—AL I:40.

Dear student, before you attempt this ritual it's important to note that Crowley has plainly stated a piece of profound wisdom, often overlooked and misunderstood by the novice. I believe the following comment should be memorized. "Those who regard this ritual as a mere device to invoke or banish spirits, are unworthy to possess it. Properly understood, it is the Medicine of Metals and the Stone of the Wise."[1] Just as this ritual effects external manifestations it also affects an individual's internal currents. As Above, So Below. Ah, yes, maybe if I repeat this phrase enough you'll always remember to relate it to all magickal principles. If a person never works

Enochian magick, nor attempts to venture into the depths of the astral waters, they would still be richly rewarded if they only did the requirements of The Magickal Diary, Liber Resh vel Helios and The Lesser Ritual of The Pentagram. The latter two rituals in particular help balance and purify an individual's internal waters. They lay a foundation whereby gross matter and astral sludge is slowly transformed into a clear spring, allowing an individual to aspire toward greater spiritual heights from which they may perceive their Star and True Will. It is said that without the proper Knowledge of these rituals one's magickal journey can be an incredibly difficult and lengthy ordeal, or even an impossible one.

In your research you may discover that there are many variations of the Banishing Ritual. These usually reflect the spiritual proclivities of individuals or certain groups. Yet of all of these, I'd suggest that beginners learn The Lesser Ritual of the Pentagram. Its origin is somewhat obscure. Traditionally the ritual is credited as being the work of Eliphas Levi although no copies of his ritual survives and there is only a brief reference to such in one of his books. The earliest recorded version of the ritual is found in the magical writings of The Hermetic Order of The Golden Dawn. Aleister Crowley learned this ritual while a Neophyte in that fraternity around 1898 and, historically, he was the first person to actually publish a version of what he learned. This occurred in 1901 when he published a rendition of the ritual in an interesting poem entitled "The Palace of the World." It appeared in a collection of his poetry entitled The Soul of Osiris. We're not concerned with breaking down this poem verse by verse at this point, we just wanted to mention its history. Still, people would be richly rewarded if they were to at least read it.

Four years after he published this poem, Crowley released the first of three volumes called The Collected Works of Aleister Crowley. Herein he included The Soul of Osiris but under a different title, calling it The Temple of The Holy Ghost. Besides the name change, there are new poems added and some old ones taken out. Crowley also added footnotes describing each section of The Palace of the World. In the footnote attached to the title of the poem Crowley writes that it "Describes the spiritual aspect of the 'Lesser Ritual of the Pentagram,' which we append, with explanation."[2] He then gives his version of The Lesser Ritual of the Pentagram, which is where the ritual was first published. A few years later he would incorporate the ritual in one of his manuscripts entitled "Liber O vel Manus et Sagittae" which appeared in The Equinox Vol. I No. 2 in 1909. It is also found in his opus Magick in Theory & Practice. If one is interested you might want to compare Crowley's version to the original Golden Dawn ritual, the latter being published by Israel Regardie in his monumental book entitled The Golden Dawn. There are slight differences. In recent years The Lesser Ritual of the Pentagram has appeared in virtually every serious book on magick. At this point I'd like to give you the ritual as it appeared in The Collected Works.

The Lesser Ritual of the Pentagram

(i.) Touching the forehead, say Ateh (Unto Thee).
(ii.) Touching the breast, say Malkuth (The Kingdom).
(iii.) Touching the right shoulder, say ve-Geburah (and the Power).
(iv.) Touching the left shoulder, say ve-Gedulah (and the Glory).
(v.) Clasping the hands upon the breast, say le-Olahm, Amen (to the Ages, Amen).
(vi.) Turning to the East, make a pentagram with the proper weapon. Say Yod He Vau He.
(vii.) Turning to the South, the same, but say Adonai.
(viii.) Turning to the West, the same, but say Ahih.
(ix.) Turning to the North, the same, but say Agla.

(x.) Extending the arms in the form of a cross, say—
(xi.) Before me Raphael,
(xii.) Behind me Gabriel,
(xiii.) On my right hand Michael,
(xiv.) On my left hand Auriel,
(xv.) for about me flames the Pentagram,
(xvi.) and in the Column stands the six-rayed Star.
(xvii.–xxi.) Repeat (i.) to (v.), the "Qabalistic Cross."

Crowley did some simple revisions to this ritual regarding sections ii and iii. However it was never published during his lifetime, being only distributed amongst OTO Initiates. In these revisions, after one touches the forehead saying Ateh, Crowley would have you "(ii) Touching the breast saying Aiwass" and then while "(iii) Touching the Genitals say Malkuth (The Kingdom)." The rest of the ritual was renumbered and remains basically the same. The general belief behind this change is to have individuals link their solar heart center of Tiphereth to the Thelemic current by acknowledging Aiwass as "a symbol of your own Holy Guardian Angel."[3] It also moves Malkuth away from your heart center to a more appropriate location, although some believe this is still wrong. The genital area is far more Yesod-Sphere 9 than Malkuth-Sphere 10 on the Tree of Life. Instead of touching the genitals I feel you should point toward your feet, thereby referring to the place where both you and the earth unite.

I can understand the logic of Crowley's changes but I do not necessarily agree with them. In fact, Grady McMurtry and I argued about this on several occasions. When I was Lodge Master back in Connecticut in the late '70s, I never taught this aspect of the Banishing Ritual even though Grady felt it was mandatory. The first time he told me this I reminded him that he hadn't sent me a copy of the ritual yet nor fully explained it. He apologized and immediately sent one in the mail. When it arrived and I saw the notes and changes, I still could not bring myself to do it. Thus, Grady and I still argued. I always believed if any name needs to be vibrated when touching the chest it should be that of your own Holy Guardian Angel or a term reflecting your aspiration toward such, even if your angel is presently unknown. It's a personal thing with me. I simply did not like using the name of another person's Guardian Angel, even if it was only a symbolic gesture. However, if you're looking for something to represent the 93 Current for your heart center then Aiwass is definitely it, as long as you realize that he is not your Holy Guardian Angel. Remember, Crowley has stated in no uncertain terms "Aiwaz is none other than mine own Holy Guardian Angel, to whose Knowledge and Conversation I have attained, so that I have exclusive access to him."[4]

To appreciate the Pentagram Ritual you must learn the symbolism behind each stage but, before this can be done, we must acknowledge that the ritual deals primarily with Self rather than universal forces, although it does have an effect on the latter. This becomes apparent by the symbolism found in the ritual itself. Let us examine the first section known as The Qabalistic Cross. You should be facing East when this part of the ritual is being performed. Then slowly "Touching the forehead," preferably with your thumb between the index and middle fingers, you vibrate "Ateh" which means 'Unto Thee.' This represents Kether, the first sphere on the Tree of Life, as well as those forces directly above the head. It properly refers to the Crown chakra and not the Ajna chakra, or Third Eye, as some people would have you think. The Ajna rules the second sphere of Chokmah. This argument stems from a misunderstanding of facts. The Crown chakra is located on top of the skull while the Ajna lies between the brows, both seemingly near the forehead. However, the key is found with the term "Ateh" or Thou Art. Qabalistically this refers to an aspect of Kether, not Chokmah, and fulfills the top of the Middle Pillar on which this section of the ritual works. This is obvious since the next stage has you inappropriately touching the genitals while vibrating

"Malkuth." This is a Hebrew word for the Kingdom which is represented by the tenth sphere on the Tree at the bottom of the Middle Pillar. Thus you are uniting one (Kether) with ten (Malkuth). As mentioned earlier, the genital area is more Yesod. You should actually be pointing toward your feet when vibrating Malkuth to signify 'Earth.'

In the second part of the Qabalistic Cross you are told to touch your right shoulder and vibrate "ve-Geburah." This means 'the Power' and refers to the fifth sphere of Geburah, or Mars, which is found on the Left-Hand Pillar. You then touch the left and vibrate "ve-Gedulah" which means 'and the Glory.' This represents the fourth sphere of Chesed, or Jupiter, and is located on the Right-Hand Pillar. Although rarely mentioned, the touching of both right and left shoulder should be done with opposite hands. This forms your arms in a Cross, over the chest and has your left arm affirming God's right and your right arm affirming his left. By utilizing these four spheres, an individual forms their astral body into a huge Cross. Some people close their eyes at this point, although it is not mandatory. You then imagine your body being filled with a bright light while slowly placing your palms together, touching your thumbs upon your chest, vibrating "le-Olahm, Amen" which means 'to the Ages, Amen' or more accurately 'forever, Amen.' This draws the entire current to the center of the Cross, which is your Heart Chakra. However, if you're holding a dagger this might be a bit difficult. The Golden Dawn version is better to do when using a dagger. Here you simply clasp your hands together with the dagger pulling it closely before your chest, saying "le-Olahm." You then unclasp your hands and slowly point the dagger straight out in front of you, saying "Amen." The drawing of the pentagram immediately follows this since the dagger is conveniently outstretched before you.

Earlier we mentioned that Eliphas Levi is presumed to be the author of this ritual because he mentioned it in one of his books. In *Transcendental Magic*, translated and published by Arthur Edward Waite in 1896, Levi cryptically writes that, "the initiate said raising his hand to his forehead, 'For thine,' then added 'is' and continuing as he brought down his hand to his breasts, 'the Kingdom,' then to the left shoulder, 'the Justice', afterwards to the right shoulder, 'and the Mercy'; then clasping his hands, he added 'Tibi sunt Malkuth et Geburah et Chesed per aeonas'—a sign of the Cross which is absolutely and magnificently Kabalistic, which the profanation of Gnosticism have lost completely to the official militant church. The Sign, made after this manner should precede and terminate the Conjuration of the Four."[5] A slightly different rendition or translation from Levi's French manuscript is as follows, "Thus for example, the initiate, raising his hand to his brow, said: 'Thine is,' then brought his hand to his breast, 'the Kingdom,' then transferred his hand to the left shoulder, 'the Power,' finally to the right shoulder, 'and the Glory'; then, joining his hands, he added 'Tibi sunt Malkuth et Geburah et Chesed per aeonas'—a sign of the Cross which is absolutely and splendidly Qabalistic, and which the profanation of the Gnosis has completely lost to the Official Church Militant. The sign made in this manner should precede and conclude the conjuration of the Four."[6] Either, or, they both imply the same thing with only a slight variation to the wording. In other words, Levi is definitely referring to the Qabalistic Cross that we have just discussed. At this point the question may never be answered whether or not Levi ever wrote a full Ritual of the Pentagram, or did the Adepts running the Golden Dawn simply elaborate his paragraph into something far more, as some believe.

When drawing the appropriate pentagram in the air it should be visualized as a flaming astral object. Magicians know whichever point of the pentagram you begin with determines whether you're using a fire, earth, air, water or spiritual force. For the novice the pentagram should always be drawn with one point upward. When a pentagram is drawn in this fashion it represents the authority of your Divine Spirit over all elemental or mundane things. If it is drawn with two points upward some believe it represents one's belief in matter as being more important than, and ruling over, the Divine Spirit. However, this view of the inverted pentagram is very simplistic and borders on being simply an Old Aeonic concept of good & evil. Yes, the inverted image of the pentagram is often depicted as being the ears and horns of the Sabbath Goat, or Satan, and refers to the tarot card of The Devil, but what have we learned in previous Epistles regarding this symbol? The true symbolism of both pentagrams becomes obvious when looking at the attributes to each point of the pentagram. The top, or single point, always represents the spirit. Which direction it points only logically represents rulership either 'over' the four elemental qualities of matter or 'below' them. Still, there is a Greater Mystery that can not be fully told in this Epistle as to why both pentagrams are correct, upright and inverted. Remember, we have previously stated that 'below' sometimes refers to 'within.' Therefore, if spirit lays within it implies godhood accepted on this plane, rather than wishful aspirations. I need say no more. An astute mind can figure it out.

When drawing an upright pentagram, the bottom left point is always attributed to Earth and the bottom right to Fire. The attributes of the two central points of the arm are, left to Air and right to Water. This fourfold structure is identical to the breakdown of each Enochian Watchtower when divided into four quarters. In the case of the Watchtowers, the fifth quality of Spirit is attributed to the Grand Cross, which not only dissects but also unites the four quarters. It is believed that every single line drawn on a Watchtower is an aspect of the spirit as it unfolds itself like a spider's web. Once you have memorized the attributes of each point of the pentagram, it is important to remember that you should always banish away from and invoke toward the force that you're working with. If you do not understand, these pentagrams are carefully drawn out for the novice in Crowley's *Liber O vel Manus et Sagittae*.

With the pentagram firmly in your imagination, you assume the god-form of the Enterer, which represents SPEECH. Stepping forward with the right foot while extending both arms outward, with head slightly lowered or, as Grady McMurtry often joked, "Just like Superman!" While moving into this position you vibrate the Holy Name "Yod-He-Vau-He" as you imagine the pentagram glowing in strength as if being charged by the magickal name. You also imagine unwanted forces locked within the Magickal Circle as being forced outward through the image. Upon finishing the vibrating you return to a standing position in the god-form of Harporcrates, or SILENCE, with left hand to your side and either your right hand clutched with index finger extended to your lips, or your thumb touching your lips with the fingers being closed as if sucking.

Although not mentioned in the ritual, you should then slowly point your right hand toward the ground and draw an imaginary line of flames toward the South, where you should stop. This is affirming your circle and some believe it astrally activates it. The next three stages are repetitive. Facing the South, do the same as you did in the East by drawing the Banishing Pentagram of Earth but this time vibrating "Adonai." Again point your right hand toward the ground and slowly draw an imaginary line of flame to the West. Here you do the same as before but vibrate "Ahih" and, finally turning to the North, you make another pentagram and vibrate "Agla." To complete this stage of the ritual you must turn, pointing your right hand toward the ground and slowly draw an imaginary line of flame back to the East. Not only does this close the circle but also it brings you to the proper position for the next stage of the rite, facing East where you began.

The four words, which are vibrated toward the quarters, need a brief explanation of their meaning. For YHVH some authorities will have you vibrate the name of God as Jehovah (pronounced YE-HO-VAH) instead of the individual Hebrew letters, Yod He Vau He. Although 'seemingly' correct, ask yourself with which interpretation of these letters you feel most comfortable. It is no secret that these four letters have numerous meanings. Just because they happen to be the four letters of the name Jehovah does not necessarily imply a connection any more than the word John has to a toilet. If you're uncomfortable with the Judaic connotations of a slave-god, especially considering what has been previously said about Abraxas and Abracadabra, then I'd suggest vibrating each letter separately. This represents the magickal formula of Fire/Earth/Air/Water as well as every attribute associated with these elemental qualities rather than the God Jehovah. Either, or, it's up to you to decide. Regarding the word ADONAI, this is simply a Hebrew word mean 'The Lord.' AHIH is Hebrew for 'I Am,' and is pronounced as E-HE-YE. As for the word AGLA, pronounced A-GI-LE-A, it is not really a word but the first four Hebrew letters of the phrase, 'Ateh Gibor Le-Olahm Adonai.' Crowley gives a rather lengthy translation of this phrase as being, "To Thee by the Power unto the Ages, O my Lord." It sounds good. However, more modern sources correctly translate it as 'Thou art Mighty Forever, O Lord.'

With the next stage of the ritual you extend your arms straight out at either side to form a Cross—while imagining your body as a glowing astral image. You then say, "Before me Raphael, Behind me Gabriel, On my right hand Michael, On my left hand Auriel, for about me flames the Pentagram, and in the Column stands the six-rayed Star." At this point utter confusion may occur, especially if you've read Aleister Crowley's "Notes on the Ritual of the Pentagram" where he states "You are supposed to be standing at the intersection of the paths of Samech and Pe. You are facing Tiphereth (the sun), thus on your right hand is Netzach (Venus), on your left hand Hod (Mercury), and behind you Yesod (the Moon)."[7] The average person, untrained in magick, may not realize the apparent contradiction so I will attempt to explain the obvious. First, there are no problems with the direction of Tiphereth and Yesod. However, when Crowley states that on your "right hand is Netzach, on your left hand Hod" there is a major discrepancy. The archangel whom you've previously acknowledged on your right hand is Michael but he is not the archangel of Netzach, he rules Hod. It is Auriel who rules Netzach. In other words, why do you acknowledge Michael and Auriel standing on your right and left in the ritual when, according to Crowley, the spheres they rule are on the opposite side where he claims you are standing?

Knowing that you're probably confused, it is important that we examine the ritual more carefully. We began with the Qabalistic Cross to strengthen ourselves internally by acknowledging ourselves as the center of our universe. We then drew pentagrams and a circle, which cleansed our area and defined our space on this plane. Logic dictates that if Tiphereth is before us in the East and represents air then behind us is Yesod, which is the watery aspect of the West. Our right side is automatically pointing toward the South and our left is pointing North. It's all very simple so far, even when you say, "On my right hand Michael, On my left hand Auriel." Yes, Michael is an archangel of Fire and at this point he should be on your right, or South. This means that Auriel, the archangel of Earth, must be on your left side, North, which, in fact, you're acknowledging that he is. The confusion comes when you realize that Crowley claims an individual is standing at the intersection of Phe and Samech, facing Tiphereth with Hod to one's left and Netzach toward on the right. We admit that all the elemental and archangel attributes to the four quarters are correct and seemingly have no flaw in relationship to this plane. It's only when the ritual is related to the spheres on the Tree of Life that befuddlement comes into play. Or does it?

The basic question is whether Crowley is referring to an internal or external Tree of Life where one is standing. To understand this you must know that some of the attributes on the macrocosmic Tree of Life are reversed when compared to the microcosmic Tree of Life in yourself. We're not quite mirror images of each other. The 'Above' attributes are always depicted on the backside of an image of a huge man Qabalistically equated with Adam Kadmon, or the universal Adam. In fact, most Qabalistic books draw their charts using this particular image of the Tree. After all, you cannot look at the face of God. It is only natural that if you were looking at the backside of Adam Kadmon, his left arm would be where the Left-Hand Pillar of the Tree is depicted and his right arm is then the Right-Hand Pillar.

The microcosmic Tree of Life depicted within you is slightly different. This Tree is always drawn on the frontal image of a man, referring to you, and because of this it is obvious that some attributes become reversed. For instance the Middle Pillar remains the same but the left and right pillars reverse sides. You acknowledge this microcosmic structure during The Qabalistic Cross by touching your right shoulder to vibrate ve-Geburah and touching your left to vibrate ve-Gedulah. This states that Geburah-5 and Hod-8 are on your right, while Chesed-4 and Netzach-7 are on your left. True understanding of how the ritual works comes into play with the following piece of knowledge. While the internal affirmations of the Qabalistic Cross are being acknowledged, the magician is symbolically standing at the intersection of Phe and Samech on the macrocosmic Tree of Life. In other words, the magician is mentally working above Malkuth, between Tiphereth-6, Yesod-9, Hod-8 and Netzach-7, to summon the forces of the archangels ruling these spheres down to the plane of Earth where he or she stands. Once they have been drawn down to Malkuth the archangels assume the correct elemental directions of this plane. It is not as complicated as it may seem.

To give you an idea of the flavor behind Crowley's poem "The Palace of the World" and its relationship to the ritual, he puts the affirmation "Before me Raphael" very poetically as "Before me dwells the Holy One, Anointed Beauty's King." Beauty is the title of Tiphereth. The other three verses are equally powerful and one might even suggest using them instead of the traditional sayings if it were not for the ritual version flowing so beautifully. After affirming that Raphael is before you, you then proclaim, "Behind me Gabriel." This is the archangel of Yesod, or the Moon, which is naturally behind you if you were facing Tiphereth. In the poem the reference is a bit lengthier, stating, "Behind me, mightier than the Sun, To whom the cherubs sing, A strong archangel, known of none, Comes crowned and conquering." Instead of saying, "On my right hand, Michael" Crowley's poem has, "An angel stands on my right hand, With strength of ocean's wrath." As a footnote to this line Crowley writes "Michael, lord of Hod, an Emanation of a watery nature." The ritual then has you acknowledging Auriel, although the poem states, "Upon my left hand the fiery brand, Charioted fires smites forth." As a footnote to this line Crowley writes, "Auriel, archangel of Netzach, to which Fire is attributed."

The wording of this section of the ritual, or any part, should not be taken lightly and, because of such, there is a part that I believe is blatantly wrong and should be corrected. This is the use of the name Auriel in the Golden Dawn version of the ritual, as reported by Aleister Crowley. I've chosen to use it up to this point rather than creating confusion too soon. According to Qabalistic lore, Auriel is one of the 72 angels who rules part of the zodiac[8] and he is not, I repeat not, an archangel, as are Michael, Gabriel and Raphael. The appropriate archangel of earth is Uriel. For instance, the correct names of the archangels who communicated with Enoch are listed in The Book of Enoch as, "Michael, Uriel, Raphael, and Gabriel."[9] John Dee also refers to them as "Michael, Gabriel, Raphael, or Uriel."[10] Additionally there is an ancient orthodox Hebrew night prayer that contains a similar reference. At the end of the prayer an individual is supposed to say, "In the name of the Lord God of Israel, may Michael be at my right hand, and Gabriel at my left, before me Uriel; behind me Raphael; and above my head the divine presence."[11] It can only be speculated whether or not the original creator of the Pentagram Ritual knew of this prayer, although the ritual does seem to have similar wording. As for the use of the name Auriel, some believe the Golden Dawn was simply confused in an attempt to use a similar angelic name of Ariel whom John Dee claims, "is a conglomerate of Anael and Uriel."[12]

Other scholars have pointed out more discrepancies. For instance, in *The Magus*[13] Uriel is mentioned as an angel ruling over only one of the four quarters of our planet, that of the South. Furthermore, according to *The Magus*, this direction, and not the traditional north, is attributed to the element of earth. Uriel's immediate angelic subordinate, who is the actual 'ruler of the element of earth' is Ariel. This same book gives the rulership of each quarter to different archangels than the accepted norm, although the rulership between angel and element is correct. For example, in the East is Fire ruled by Michael, the West is Air ruled by Raphael, the North is water ruled by Gabriel and, as I just pointed out, the South is Earth ruled by Uriel. The bottom line is this, angelic research is a bitch of contradiction and will lead a person down a path of befuddlement. Regardless of when or how the original confusion occurred regarding the name Auriel, I would suggest that one uses the correct name of Uriel when performing the Pentagram Ritual.

There is a Greater Mystery that can only be grasped if you clearly understood what was said in previous Epistles regarding the union of opposites and the fourfold direction just mentioned. Previously we stated that when Chokmah and Binah unite a Hidden Door (Daleth) is opened which allows an influence to descend upon Tiphereth and then to manifest through it while riding the elemental tides. Once it begins to descend it approaches the magician who, when beginning the performance of the Lesser Ritual of the Pentagram, is facing East toward Tiphereth or the Sun. In this ritual the process of Babalon and the Beast conjoined takes place within an individual. It begins the final completion of an individual's 'transformation' and now we can begin to understand why Crowley wrote "Those who regard this ritual as a mere device to invoke or banish spirits, are unworthy to possess it. Properly understood, it is the Medicine of Metals and the Stone of the Wise."

The path that is most crucial at this stage is known as Art, or Alchemy. It is the final ON as taught in Seventh Degree OTO. In Epistle No. 7 An Open Letter on obtaining the Knowledge we stated, "There are other Mysteries too Divine to be openly discussed in this particular Epistle but I will tell you this, Crowley has stated that the Minerval Word of ON works within The Devil card and is fulfilled in its final alchemical stage when an individual enters the Hermetic Triad as a Seventh Degree whose Word is also ON. This final stage is depicted by the Thoth card of Art which is attributed to the Hebrew letter Samech-60 and is ruled by Sagittarius. Why these two particular cards refer to these two OTO Degree Words might be difficult to understand. However, Crowley plainly gives this knowledge before the eyes of the profane in "Liber 777" Col. CLXXXVII on 'Magical Formulae' but without clear indication as to how these attributes relate to the magical formula of ON. Still, with all that we've already discussed regarding The Devil card it should not be difficult to figure out its relationship to Minerval Degree with just a fair amount of meditation. The path of Art may be a bit difficult to grasp regarding Seventh Degree but the Pentagram Ritual will unfold these mysteries when we discuss this in a later Epistle. This is why in the past every Minerval was informed that they must learn this ritual but, with regret, this obligation is no longer being officially taught within OTO." Now do you understand? I wish to reiterate what I just previously stated. This is the path which an influence, or entity, like one's Holy Guardian Angel, uses to manifest once it has been drawn through the Sun. This is critical to realize. An alchemical drawing of a Hermaphrodite, half man and half woman often portrays the card of Art, as if to imply both Left-Hand (418) and Right-Hand (156) Pillars have merged together, as the Sun and Moon do through the Middle Path or Pillar. The words 'Middle Path' when using English Qabalah add to 574. 418+156 = 574. This merging is you and your angel.

In a previous Epistle I've already discussed the combination of the two ancient magickal principles of Sun and Moon. The Solar quality, referred to as 666, represents the material world uniting with the Lunar quality of 1080, being the Holy Spirit, and how you should consider the solar principle (fire) and the Lunar principle (water) as circles, similar to the triangles of the Holy Hexagram. I mentioned how when these two circles intersect they create an ancient symbol known as the Vesica Piscis, often referred to as The Vessel of Pisces. Has a light bulb gone off yet? The magician is standing in the center of this image of intersecting circles between Sun (Tiphereth) and Moon (Yesod) when performing the Lesser Ritual of the Pentagram.

To reflect upon this further one needs only to realize that after acknowledging the four archangels you loudly proclaim, "for about me flames the Pentagram, and in the Column stands the six-rayed Star." Besides the obvious, that the blending of 'five' and 'six' equals 'eleven' and is a reference to the Great Work. The six-rayed Star refers to the fact that if the ritual is performed correctly a Holy Hexagram automatically appears. This symbol in itself also portrays the union of opposites that we've been discussing all along. Crowley has noted that you "are thus standing in a Column which is protected by your microcosmic invocation. The consequent result, being macrocosmic response, is that without any effort on your part the hexagram or six-fold star appears both above and below you."[14] In other words the column refers not only to your 'microcosmic' spinal column, which is the primary energy channel between your chakras but also the 'macrocosm' of the central pillar on the Tree of Life. In the center of both columns is Tiphereth, the sixth sphere. This solar attribute is further expressed at the very end of the ritual when you clasp your hands upon your chest vibrating "le-Olahm, Amen." On a microcosmic level what you've acknowledged is that your central Star, or Sun, exists as portrayed by the Holy Hexagram, which is a symbol of ABRAHADABRA 418. Also, the elemental forces that stream forth within its rays can be affected by yourself and can affect your spiritual 'transformation' at the same time. The illusions that bind humanity have no hold on you. You are in complete control of those forces depicted in The Devil trump of the tarot. The waters that once ran muddy and stagnant can now become clear around your tiny island. Burn into your mind these verses from Chapter Three of *The Book of the Law*, "Choose ye an island!" "Fortify it!" Those words, as well as the following which Crowley wrote, I'd like to repeat one last time because they should echo in your mind whenever you perform a Pentagram Ritual. "Those who regard this ritual as a mere device to invoke or banish spirits, are unworthy to possess it. Properly understood, it is the Medicine of Metals and the Stone of the Wise."

Further study reveals there are numerous slight variations and theories behind the subtleties portrayed in the Pentagram Ritual. Many are correct and portray the personal proclivities of individuals who understand the ritual and have fine-tuned it to suit their beliefs. This is perfectly all right, yet to do this successfully you must know not only the symbolism behind the ritual but also the magickal mechanism which makes it work. This ritual, like the variations, may seem complicated but if one were to understand the principle they could virtually forget the lengthy and almost verbose rite and do something far simpler. In fact, Crowley has stated that *The Book of The*

Law contains all the Supreme Formulas and therefore this rite "may now advantageously be replaced by (a single verse and that being) 'pure will unassuaged of purpose, delivered from the lust of result, is every way perfect' (CCXX I:44) to banish."[15] As simple as this sounds it is far more complicated to use than doing the full Lesser Ritual of the Pentagram. However, I have given every clue on how this simple verse can work in the pages of this Epistle. Crowley has also rewritten The Banishing Ritual of the Pentagram into a totally different format, which he claims "is the best to use."[16] This appeared in *Liber 333, The Book of Lies*, Chapter 25 and is titled The Star Ruby. It is also found in *Magick in Theory & Practice*. I am not going into all the theory behind this ritual or its symbolism. I personally feel the elemental formulas regarding the Pentagram Ritual that I've already discussed are best for the beginner.

Anyway, after all has been said and done, you might wonder how you will know if what you're doing is correct. Israel Regardie said it best when he wrote, "There should be a clear sense, unmistakable in its manifestation, as of cleanliness, even holiness and sanctity, as though the whole being were gently but thoroughly purged, and that every impure and unclean element had been dispersed and annihilated."[17] Crowley further adds that, "a sign that the student is performing this correctly (is) when a single 'Vibration' entirely exhausts his physical strength. It should cause him to grow hot all over or to perspire violently, and it should so weaken him that he will find it difficult to remain standing."[18] Yet he shall remain standing and because he's practiced the ritual he will continue with the next stage. Yes, it is no secret that performing this ritual affects both the individual and his surroundings. I can attest that the atmosphere definitely changes and is noticeable by everyone, especially in Temples where the ritual is continually performed. There are only a few things I'd like to end this chapter with. The first is to remind the student to invoke often and then to quote Crowley, who equally warns his students, "Neglect not the Performance of the Ritual of the Pentagram."[19] Finally, I'd like to include one of Crowley's poems that I hope will give further inspiration.

The Pentagram[20]

In the years of the Primal Course,
in the dawn of terrestrial birth,
Man mastered the mammoth and horse,
and Man was the Lord of the Earth.

He made him an hollow skin
from the heart of an holy tree,
He compassed the earth therein,
and Man was the Lord of the Sea.

He controlled the vigour of steam,
he harnessed the lightning for hire;
He drove the celestial team;
and Man was the Lord of the Fire.

Deep-mouthed from their thrones deep-seated,
the choirs of the aeons declare
The last of the demons defeated,
for Man is the Lord of the Air.

Arise, O Man, in thy strength!
the kingdom is thine to inherit,
Till the high gods witness at length
that Man is the Lord of his spirit.

Love is the law, love under will.—AL I:57.

NOTES

[1]Aleister Crowley, "The Temple of the Holy Ghost, The Palace of the World," *The Collected Works, Volume 1*, 1905 (New York: Gordon Press, 1974), footnote no. 1, p. 204.

[2]Crowley, *Collected Works*, Vol. 1, p. 204.

[3]Soror Meral, *In The Continuum Vol. 1 No. 1* (California: The College of Thelema, 1973), p. 2.

[4]Aleister Crowley, *The Equinox of the Gods* (London: Privately printed by OTO, 1936), p. 127.

[5]Eliphas Levi, *Transcendental Magic*, trans. Arthur Edward Waite (New York: Samuel Weiser, Inc., 1974) p. 234.

[6]Francis King, *Astral Projection* (New York: Samuel Weiser, Inc., 1975), p. 23.

[7]Soror Meral, p. 6.

[8]Dagobert Runes, *The Wisdom of the Kabbalah* (New York: Philosophical Library, 1957).

[9]*The Book of Enoch*, trans. R.H. Charles (Oxford: Claredon Press, 1912), Chapter IX, Verse 1, p. 20.

[10]John Dee, *The Private Diary of John Dee*, ed. James Orchard Halliwell (London: The Camden Society, 1842), p. 22.

[11]*Daily Prayer Book, Ha-Siddur Ha-Shalem*, trans. Philip Birnbaum (New York: Hebrew Publishing Company, no date), p. 852.

[12]Gustav Davidson, *A Dictionary of Angels*, including The Fallen Angels (New York: The Free Press, 1967), p. 54.

[13]Francis Barrett, *The Magus, Book I* (New York: University Books, New Hyde Park, 1967) p. 112.

[14]Soror Meral, p. 6.

[15]Aleister Crowley, *Magick In Theory & Practice* (New Jersey: Castle Press, 1965) p. 107.

[16]*Ibid.*, p. 104.

[17]Israel Regardie, *The Tree of Life* (New York: Samuel Weiser, Inc., 1969) p. 167.

[18]Crowley, *Magick In Theory & Practice* p. 379.

[19]Aleister Crowley, *Liber Aleph*, (San Francisco: Level Press, 1972) p. 16.

[20]Aleister Crowley, *The Winged Beetle* (London: privately printed, 1910), p. 149.

fh FERAL HOUSE www.feralhouse.com

"The most courageous and incendiary publisher in the U.S." —*Headpress*

SEX AND ROCKETS: The Occult World of Jack Parsons

John Carter; Introduction by Robert Anton Wilson

By day, John Whiteside "Jack" Parsons co-founded the Jet Propulsion Laboratory and the Aerojet Corporation. His unorthodox genius created a solid rocket fuel that helped win World War II and send spacecraft to the moon. By night, Parsons called himself The Antichrist when he performed Aleister Crowley's Thelemic rituals to create a new sort of human that would finally destroy Christianity. At 37, Jack Parsons died in a huge explosion that cannot be definitively explained. Was it murder? Suicide? Or just an accident?

• Updated Paperback Edition with new photos and Afterword
• 5 1/2 x 8 1/2 • 239 pages • illustrated • $16.95 • ISBN: 0-922915-97-0

ORGASMATRON: The Heavy Metal Art of Joe Petagno

Joe Petagno; Foreword by Lemmy Kilmister; Introduction by Steffan Chirazi

Joe Petagno's iconographic covers for the hard rock band Mötorhead are only a small part of his prolific painting career. Starting out with the renowned Hipgnosis, designing for Led Zeppelin and Pink Floyd, this book emphasizes Petagno's work for heavy metal recordings and paintings seen only in his Denmark home. *Orgasmatron: The Heavy Metal Art of Joe Petagno* goes where no art book has ever gone before.

• 9 x 9 • 108 pages • hardcover • color • $19.95 • ISBN: 1-932595-00-7

LORDS OF CHAOS:
The Bloody Rise of the Satanic Metal Underground

Michael Moynihan and Didrik Søderlind

"An unusual combination of true crime journalism, rock and roll reporting and underground obsessiveness, *Lords of Chaos* turns into one of the more fascinating reads in a long time..." —David Thomas, *Denver Post*

"Gripping stuff, a book about scary rock that is really scary." —Mike Tribby, *Booklist*

Lords of Chaos won the Firecracker Award for Best Music Book of 1998.

• Newly updated and expanded edition
• 6 x 9 • 404 pages • illustrated • $18.95 • ISBN: 0-922915-94-6

TO ORDER FROM FERAL HOUSE: Domestic orders add $4.50 shipping for first item, $2.00 each additional item. AmEx, MasterCard, Visa, checks and money orders are accepted. (CA state residents add 8.25% tax.) Canadian orders add $9 shipping for first item, $6 each additional item. Other countries add $11 shipping for first item, $9 each additional item. Non-U.S. originated orders must be international money order or check drawn on a U.S. bank only. Send orders to: *Feral House, P.O. Box 39910, Los Angeles, CA 90039.* Orders can also be placed at *www.feralhouse.com*.